Hot
MAMA

Books by Kathi Lipp and Erin MacPherson

10 Ideas to Inspire Red Hot Sex (ebook)

10 Quick Fashion Fixes to Feel Confident and Sexy (ebook)

10 Hot Date Night Ideas for Married Couples (ebook)

Hot Mama

Hot
MAMA

12 SECRETS TO A
sizzling hot MARRIAGE

—

KATHI LIPP
AND ERIN MACPHERSON

Revell

a division of Baker Publishing Group
Grand Rapids, Michigan

© 2015 by Kathi Lipp and Erin MacPherson

Published by Revell
a division of Baker Publishing Group
P.O. Box 6287, Grand Rapids, MI 49516-6287
www.revellbooks.com

Printed in the United States of America

Library of Congress Cataloging-in-Publication Data
Lipp, Kathi, 1967–
    Hot mama : 12 secrets to a sizzling hot marriage / Kathi Lipp and Erin MacPherson.
        pages cm
    Includes bibliographical references.
    ISBN 978-0-8007-2677-5 (pbk.)
    1. Sex in marriage—Religious aspects—Christianity. I. Title.
BT708.L57 2015
248.8′435—dc23   2015010387

Published in association with the Books & Such Literary Management, 52 Mission Circle, Suite 122, PMB 170, Santa Rosa, CA 95409-5370, www.booksandsuch.com

To protect the privacy of those who have shared their stories with the authors, some details and names have been changed.

15 16 17 18 19 20 21   7 6 5 4 3 2 1

Contents

Acknowledgments   7

Introduction   9

1. The Hot Mama Way   13
2. Thou Shalt Enjoy Sex   18
3. Confidence Is Key   27
4. Throw Out the Guilt   37
5. Hot Dates over Playdates   48
6. Getting over Our Good Girl Issues   59
7. Get in the Mood   69
8. Let's Talk about Sex, Baby   77
9. Speak Respect   87
10. Keep Sex out of the Locker Room   96
11. Heat Things Up   105
12. Knowing Your Man   114

13. What Happens in the Bedroom, Happens in
Our Bedroom   123

Bonus Section:

Ask Our Sexperts   135

Girlfriend-to-Girlfriend Q&A   159

More Tips from Real Hot Mamas   179

Continuing Your Hot Mama Journey   183

Notes   185

Acknowledgments

This book started with a tribe—a group of hot mamas, who like us, wanted to make their marriages hot and honor God in the process. There is not enough chocolate in the world to express our gratitude to our hot mama team, so we'll start with a heaping dose of acknowledgment right here.

Thank you to the hundreds of women who contributed to this book in one way or another. Special thanks to Robyn Arnold, Christy Ahart, Mollie Burpo, Lori Callister, Melissa Carter, Laura Choy, Sarah Craven, Emily Deiss, Alisa Dusan, Sandy Fivecoat, Susy Flory, Cheri Gregory, Connie Hagen, Michelle Halvorsen, Annie Hoffman, Hannah Hudson, Laura Jennings, Katie Kessel, Laura Marion-Faul, Shannon Martin, Sharon McCaskill, Dina Morris, Rebecca Palmer, Mollie Pierce, Rachel Randolph, Sue Alice Sauthoff, Monica Scantlon, Stevi Schuknecht, Bianca Vimont, and Sarah Windham for being the best hot mama friends we could ask for. For giving us stories, ideas, fuel, and friendship. We love you all.

Acknowledgments

We also want to acknowledge our expert team who gave us the answers to the questions that all of our hot mama friends kept asking. Thank you to Bonny Logsdon Burns, Paul and Lori Byerly, Jay Dee, Bill Gionovetti, Dr. Jeff Hagen, Rob Harrell, Mike Kaylani, Virginia Mosby, and Lucille Zimmerman. We are so blessed by amazing professional counselors, pastors, and doctors like you who love God and love people and are willing to share your expertise.

Thank you to our wonderful publishing team, both at Books & Such Literary and at Revell. We couldn't be more thrilled to work with such a talented, fun, and savvy team.

And last but certainly not least, we thank our respective husbands, Roger and Cameron, who not only put up with long hours and PB&J dinners while we wrote this book but also supported us 100 percent as we embarked on a journey to talk about sex in public. You both deserve a medal. And a big heaping dose of King Ranch chicken casserole.

Introduction

(Erin)

I was wearing yoga pants.

And not the cool Lululemon kind of yoga pants, but the ratty grey kind that I had picked up at Target eight years ago before they carried Lululemon knockoffs.

But my friend N was wearing jeans. Real, buttonable jeans. And a cute shirt. And . . . wait for it . . . lipstick.

Now, I'm not one to judge, but who wears lipstick to preschool drop-off?

Anyway, after N and I dropped off our kids, we headed to Whole Foods to have coffee and chat. We sat there sipping our lattes and talking life when N's phone buzzed.

She picked it up and giggled.

"My husband," she said, blushing.

Five minutes later, it buzzed again. She giggled again.

A half hour later, she looked up at me and said, "Hey, this has been fun, but I . . . uh . . . gotta go." Then she held up her phone and showed me a text message from her husband.

It said, "NOONER?" (in all caps).

My mouth dropped open. A nooner? On a school day? How risqué. How totally unlike anything I had ever done. How . . . awesome.

I'm not trying to imply that my married-with-kids sex life isn't risqué and romantic and awesome . . . but, well, if I'm being honest, it's not. And can you blame me? I have three kids under eight, a job, a mortgage, and a golden retriever who sheds what seems like an entire dog's worth of fur onto my floor every day. I'm exhausted and droopy and cranky and there are times that it's easier to just throw on a pair of yoga pants and frump the night away.

But that morning at Whole Foods I saw something different.

Because N, in all of her lipstick-wearing, nooner-having glory, also has three kids. And a mortgage. And an energy-sucking, exhaustion-causing schedule that looks very similar to mine. Yet she still manages to do crazy hot mama things like wear lipstick and have sex with her husband. A lot.

Which begs the question: What do we as Christian women want from our marriages? And more importantly, what does God want? Do you think boring, ho-hum relationships that are only fulfilling when we are well rested and have a baby-sitter are what God intended when he created the most important human relationship?

I don't think so.

And neither does Kathi. Which is why after much back-and-forth chatter about marriage, relationships, and yes, even sex, Kathi and I decided to write this book. Because we know that God calls us to more than lukewarm when it comes to our relationships with our husbands. And because we also know that with the pressures of life as a mom, many

Christian marriages cool off. And when Christian moms start spending more time playing with Hot Wheels and making hot chocolate than wearing hot lingerie, there's a problem.

We don't want that!

And so, we asked our hot mama friends—you know, the ones who are making out instead of making lunch, and rushing home from coffee dates for sex—what they do to keep their marriages hot. And let me tell you, they answered. The pages of this book are filled with creative, romantic, and hot come-hither ideas, romantic stories, and even confidence-building thoughts so that you, too, can become a hot mama and build a marriage that would make other people blush. Each chapter also includes a Hot Mama Pledge, to remind us all of what we really want as wives. Copy these, highlight them, pin them, place one in your lingerie drawer—put them wherever you need a reminder of what you're after as a hot mama.

And in doing so, you'll build a marriage that's God-honoring, romantic, fun, and . . . hot.

1

The Hot Mama Way

(Kathi)

I'd venture to guess that most of you reading this would love to have a hot marriage.

But I'd also guess most of you are feeling anything but hot right now.

And is it any wonder you are not feeling like *all that*?

On TV you can't watch anything without the Victoria's Secret Angels thrusting their bustlines in your face (not to mention the face of your husband). Every magazine plays on our insecurities: we're not thin enough, mom enough, rich enough, or sexy enough. Every "reality" show says reality is having your hair and makeup professionally done every day.

We normal girls don't have a chance.

Which means we're left feeling totally unconfident, completely unsexy, and entirely unhopeful that we could ever be a hot mama with a hot marriage and a hot sex life. When we're living with this lack of confidence, it's easy to swing to what I like to call *the mommy extreme*.

You've probably been there (or may be living there right at this very minute). This is the place where your life is overrun with the process of mothering. Pajamas are worn into the afternoon hours of the day. Clothes are given the sniff test to see if they can pass one more wearing. Dinner is a phone call to your husband on the way home and a discussion of your favorite drive-thru options. The only hot you feel is "hot mess."

There is a better way!

Remember when you were dating your husband? I bet that was a time you felt the most confident, the prettiest, and (may I be so bold to say) the sexiest. You spent a lot of time thinking about, prepping for, primping for, and getting excited about seeing your man.

And because you knew he was thinking about you, you had confidence. You were probably working or going to school at the same time, and you made it work. You found the time to be in love, work, study, and talk to your friends (and eventually, plan a wedding) all at the same time.

But then life happened. And somewhere between happily-ever-after and right now, you lost that swagger that told you to slip on those skimpy red panties and give your hubby a come-hither look. Maybe you lost your confidence. Perhaps you gained a few pounds in all the wrong places. Maybe your relationship started to struggle. Or maybe you just started to feel overwhelmed with kids and life and lost your desire.

Sex became . . . different. Not bad, per se, but different. More ho-hum. More routine. More between-the-white-cotton-sheets. And less intimate. Less exciting. Less hot.

We want to help all of our hot mama friends bring back that loving feeling. We know you have kids (and a mountain of laundry) underfoot, you're tired, and you haven't been able to pee alone for the last four years. But we also know that your marriage is important.

And so are you.

The Hot Mama Way

The secret to being hot—and a mama—is what we call the Hot Mama Way. It's about taking the confidence you had when you were dating, mixing it with the nurturing and wisdom you now have as a mom, and pouring all that newfound hot mama-ness into your relationship with your husband. It's about knowing the person God created you to be and living that out.

A hot mama knows she was joined with her husband as part of God's perfect plan for her life, and because of that, her marriage has to be her most important human relationship. She confidently pours into her marriage—striving to give her husband a safe place to land, a caring home, and a fulfilling sex life to look forward to.

That's what this book is all about—not just sex, not just marriage, not just motherhood, but how moms can intentionally and purposefully invest in all three so that they can, in turn, become the women that God wants them to be and have the relationships that God wants them to have.

The reason I love the term *hot mama* is because it reminds me that while I'm a mom and I love my kids, my role as a mom is still secondary to my role as a wife. By fulfilling that primary role intentionally, purposefully, and passionately, I am being the woman that God wants me to be (and having a lot of fun in the process).

Being a hot mama is pretty awesome, and our prayer for this book is that you'll walk away from reading it feeling both refreshed and energized, saying,

- I want my husband to walk confidently in the world knowing that he is loved by me and that I'm his biggest fan.
- I want him to know that while I love being a mom (most days) my most important role is as his wife.
- I want to have a sex life that is as fulfilling as it is fun, as passionate as it is intimate.
- I want the world to know my priorities: God, my husband, and then my kids.
- I want to hang out with other women who are also working to have better marriages and encourage them in the process.
- I want my kids to see that husband and wife is the most important relationship in this house.
- I want to get rid of the guilt I feel over things in my past, the mistakes I have made, and my areas of inadequacy. I don't want that guilt to affect my marriage.
- I want our kids to feel secure because their mom and dad's marriage is secure.

Do you want those things? I know you do.

But here's the thing: building a hot married-with-kids sex life is hard. Really hard.

Because the kids, they have a tendency to take over our lives. And that's why we hot mamas are bucking the system.

We are saying no to Mommy Martyrdom and yes to our husbands (instead of faking a headache).

How would it feel to know that you are doing everything you can to encourage your husband on a daily basis?

How would it feel if physical intimacy was just that—intimate?

How would you feel knowing that you're giving your kids a great role model of the kind of marriage they can have?

You would feel great. Let's get started.

2

Thou Shalt Enjoy Sex

May your fountain be blessed,
and may you rejoice in the wife of your
youth.

Proverbs 5:18

(Erin)

There are just so many "thou shalts" when it comes to sex.

If you aren't married, then thou shalt never think about sex at all. But if you are married, well, then thou shalt not only think about it, but thou shalt do it whenever your husband reaches over with *that* look in his eye. Thou shalt be willing. Thou shalt be awe-inspiring. Thou shalt be able to manage a life and a job and four kids who are constantly pawing at you while still being able to put on a smile and a wink for your husband and . . .

Can I just say I've about had enough of all of the thou-shalting? I'm tired of our sex-crazed society intersecting with our sex-confused church and turning what God created as a wonderful gift between husband and wife into a jumbled and confusing mess of guilt, pain, emotional drama, and—dare I say it?—rules.

I'm worn out from it.

And if I'm being honest, my sex life is getting worn out from it. It's like all the rules and shoulds and shouldn'ts have clouded our vision for what sex really could be, leaving me confused, lonely, and honestly, feeling like I'm too tired to put my cute undies on. And I don't want that!

I'm ready to look past all of the messy misconceptions we've come to associate with sex and get to the root of the issue: God made sex. For us. We may have gotten his original plan messed up in a million different ways, but if we go back to the plain truth of the matter, sex is a gift God has given us. To strengthen our marriages. To bring enjoyment. To build intimacy. To give us something fun to do on a Saturday night when it's raining outside and we have no money to pay a babysitter so we can go out on a date night.

Yes. God made sex for us.

Let's aim to see sex for what it really is: a wonderful gift that can lead to emotional fulfillment, stronger marriages, and a whole lot of fun. Would you like to join me? The pages of this book—and especially this chapter—are aimed at help-ing Christian moms see sex for what God truly intended it to be so that they can break free of the bondage that comes from human distortion of God's gift and start to truly enjoy sex. Here's how we can get started.

The Way God Sees Sex

I know I'm stating the obvious when I tell you that the world has it wrong about sex. And not just the secular world and the media, but also the church and Christian organizations. Yes, we as humans have really messed up God's gift of sex— and in doing so we have robbed ourselves of the pleasure, intimacy, and enjoyment that God intended for us.

But our God has overcome the world—which means that no matter how many people have objectified his intentions, he will not let his plans be pushed aside. Yes, that's right, no matter how many movie producers have portrayed sex incorrectly and no matter how many churches have filled kids' ears with legalistic rules, the fact remains: sex belongs to God. And because of that, we simply have to ask him and listen if we want to bring it back to where he intended it to be.

I'll be the first to admit that I entered my marriage with a completely distorted view on sex. We'll get into this more in chapter 4, but I entered my marriage thinking sex was bad. I had been indoctrinated early with the "thou shalt not think about sex" principle. I had been taught from a young age that good girls don't have sex, like sex, think about sex, or talk about sex.

It's interesting, because while I was actually a pretty rebellious teenager, sexual purity was one of those things that I was stalwart about. Not because of my stellar morals or my amazing fortitude, but because I had this idea that sex was dirty. If I partook in it, I would be dirty too.

This may have been a helpful thing when I was a teenager, but it became a negative when I got married. Instead of looking forward to my wedding night, realizing that God had created sex as an intimate expression between husband and wife, I dreaded it. And instead of enjoying my honeymoon and getting to know my husband in a way that we hadn't been able to before, I spent a lot of time feeling guilt-ridden and dirty because I was doing something that, well, good girls didn't do.

I've (obviously) worked past that (thank you, good Christian counselors), but my preconceived notions about sex were really damaging to our early relationship. And I'd venture to guess that the preconceived notions of many women— whether they were learned from parents, movies, magazines, books, or friends—have been damaging to their marriages.

You can't change the way you were taught about sex, and you certainly can't change the stigmas that come with the "thou shalts" or the "you shoulds" that you've heard about sex, but you can start to look at sex differently and in the way God sees it.

The first place I would start is the Bible—see what God has to say about the marital relationship and see how you've misconstrued those truths. I would start with 1 Corinthians 13 and Song of Solomon, and move on to Proverbs 5, 1 Corinthians 6, and Ephesians 5. After reading these passages, ask yourself some honest questions. How do you view sex? Where does your viewpoint align with God's and where does it stray from his? How has society and the church affected your sex life? This will take some careful examining—in some cases, you may need to turn to a professional counselor to work through your own misconceptions—but I believe that with honest reflection and prayer, you will see the truth in how our world has distorted God's design. And how inherently perfect his design is.

Using Sex to Strengthen Your Marriage

I'd be willing to go out on a limb and say that it's virtually impossible to have a strong marriage without a good sex life. Why? Because sex is the one thing that sets your marriage relationship apart from every other relationship you have—it's the one thing you can give to your husband that's only his and the one thing he can give you that's only yours. It's the one way you can connect in a way that's emotional, spiritual, and physical all at once. It's intimate and passionate and . . . important.

Since I've already ascertained that couples with strong marriages generally have a good sex life, it's just a short leap to conclude that couples who work on building their sex lives are also strengthening their marriages in the process. And, couples who work consistently and diligently on their marriages are seeking God in their relationships. So by snuggling up to your hubby tonight and kissing him passionately, you are doing God's work. Makes total sense, right?

In all seriousness, sex is a great marriage builder. If you feel like your relationship has started to drift, one of the best ways to get it back on track is to work on your sex life. Because I believe that if a couple has a satisfying and intimate sex life, they will naturally be able to be intimate and honest in other areas of their lives.

How Sex Can Heal

My husband and I got in a huge fight over the clothes dryer—yes, the clothes dryer—a few weeks ago. Our heating element broke, and after a three-hour attempt to fix it, my husband realized the repair was beyond his handyman skills. He said he was going to call for help. Now, in my mind, that meant he was going to call a more qualified handyman in, say, five minutes. But in his mind, it meant he was going to call a more qualified handyman when he had the time. Which may have taken a bit longer than I would have liked.

Let's just say I let him know I wasn't happy. And through a pile of sopping-wet laundry that I was hauling to the car to dry at my mom's house, I might have told him how I felt. And he might have snapped back that he was busy and I needed to be patient. And ten minutes later—well, let's just say that some wet socks were thrown and some choice words were uttered.

I marched in the door armed with a mouthful of reasons why I was angry. And I was stopped in my tracks with a kiss as my husband swooped me off to bed. It's hard to stay angry with someone when you're having sex with them—and it's hard to stay fractured when you're connecting on a deep and intimate level.

Now, I'm not saying that you should have sex every time you're angry with each other—trust me, there are some fights that can only heal with conversation (or even counseling) and a huge bowl of Dove chocolates. But sometimes—especially when the fight is emotionally charged or (dare I say?) irrational—sex can be the best medicine. When appropriate, sex can be a means to heal wounds that probably shouldn't have been scratched open to begin with.

The Gift of Intimacy

Think about the last time you had sex with your husband. Think about how you felt afterward—snuggled up next to him all warm and flushed and safe in his arms. It felt nice, right? Like you had connected powerfully and on a level that most human relationships can't touch. That type of honest, open, passionate, and safe intimacy is what God designed for the marriage relationship. And that kind of intimacy is something that hot mamas crave.

I think many women realize that physical intimacy can lead to intimacy in all areas of life—but it takes a certain level of confidence and finesse for a mama to grab that intimacy by the horns and . . . well, make it happen for herself. Reading this book is a great start—you are admitting that it takes hard work to build intimacy. But we want to challenge you to continue the quest so that you can have a fulfilled, close, and intimate marriage.

A *Hot Mama* PLEDGE

I want to enjoy sex, so I will

- prayerfully work to get rid of the harmful preconceived notions that I have about sex, allowing myself to see sex in the way God sees it.

- not allow societal influences to affect my sex life.

- let my husband know that I desire an emotionally and physically intimate life with him and that I'm willing to work toward that.

- allow my sex life to be fun, energetic, engaging, and godly.

REAL *Hot Mama* IDEAS

"My husband and I read Song of Solomon together at night and discuss the differences between how our world views sex and how God does. It's been so great to gain a true understanding of sex from a biblical perspective and to be able to confidently know that God didn't design the sex-crazed and sex-fueled culture that is so prevalent."—T

"After a discussion about the world's distorted view of sex at our MOPS table, my friends and I decided to 'fast' from worldly sex so we can 'feast' on what God truly intended for us. That means we made a pact to avoid women's magazines, books, movies, and TV programs that objectify sex, and instead focus on what God really intended for sex."—K

"I grew up in a really (really) strict home where sex wasn't talked about at all. I entered my marriage completely unsure of what God intended for sex. I do not want that to happen to my daughter, so I checked out *Simple Truths* by Mary Flo Ridley and am actively praying about how I can raise my children to understand God's definition of sex instead of the world's."—N

Hot Mama
"Enjoy Sex" BUCKET LIST

1. Initiate sex with your husband. Go up to him (yes, right now) and give him a little wink, wink, nudge, nudge and let him know that you want to have sex with him—because it's fun and you want to and for no other reason.

2. Write your husband a letter letting him know how much your sex life means to you.

3. Read through Song of Solomon and reflect on God's design for sex.

4. Have make-up sex. Next time you are in an argument with your husband, turn to him and kiss him passionately, and in doing so, let him know that sex can be a bridge to bring that intimacy back.

5. Ban damaging media from your entertainment repertoire. (For the record, we're not telling you to stop watching TV or reading books—but instead, to recognize the programs and literature that are damaging to your perspective and remove them from your life.)

6. Have a conversation with your husband about sex. Let him know how much you enjoy it.

7. Make an intentional effort to have sex at least three times a week for the next month. Make a mental note of how much you like having it.

3

Confidence Is Key

For you formed my inward parts;
> you knitted me together in my mother's
> womb.
I praise you, for I am fearfully and wonderfully
> made.
Wonderful are your works;
> my soul knows it very well.

Psalm 139:13–14 ESV

(Kathi)

"I can't wait to see you naked."

Seven dreaded words. Worse than "I have an idea! Let's go camping!" or "There's a Star Wars movie opening today!" I hated those words.

Roger and I were engaged, and, unlike my first marriage, Roger and I were waiting until we were married to have sex. But that didn't mean that it wasn't a huge topic of conversation (and one of the main reasons we had a mere six-week engagement).

And I was excited to be that intimate with Roger. But if he ever thought that we were going to be in the same room, naked, at the same time, with the lights on, he was out of his ever-loving mind. I had a lot working against me:

1. I've had two babies. Things that used to stay in place while having sex were certainly going to have a mind of their own. The thought of the jiggling, wiggling, and possible whiplash I could cause my future husband scared me.

2. I've been overweight since I was three. We're not talking ten extra pounds my first year of college. My stomach is no longer a smooth surface. Thanks to stretch marks, it resembles a three-year-old's self-portrait. Not pretty.

3. Gravity. Enough said.

Add to that the fact that Roger had been married before. He had someone to compare me to. Awesome, right?

So while I was beside-myself-excited to be married to Roger, I wondered if there was any way that I could go through our marriage sleeping in a Spanx full-body suit.

But clearly, Roger was having none of it.

Actually, that's not true. Roger wanted all of it. About a week before we were married, I opened up to him about my fear of getting naked. "I'm sure you're going to be disappointed in what you see."

Roger told me that wasn't true. He was excited to get to know me—even the parts of me that I felt unconfident about.

Because of this (and because I so badly wanted to make this marriage work on every level), I needed to figure out sex with the lights on. And I needed to get over my body insecurities that seemed to creep up every time I thought about being intimate with him. After we were married, we wouldn't be getting away with romantic candlelight while we were getting dressed for work each day. Plus, I knew that a big part of having a great sex life was that I actually, sometimes, felt sexy.

So after we married, I asked Roger if we could take things slowly. Dark rooms, killer lingerie, and sheets were all part of my take-it-slow plan. Oh yes! We still had sex—it was just the full visual that I had a hard time with. He didn't completely understand, but I explained that I would definitely feel more sexy if I didn't imagine him tracing the lines of stretch marks in his mind.

I also told him to let me know what was important to him. He let me know that yes, the visual was important, but for him, physical touch was the most important aspect of sex. I made sure that I concentrated my efforts in what mattered the most. He gave me an A in this area.

Finally, I told Roger what I needed. I told him that I needed him to let me know what aspects of my body turned him on. (Yes—it was a very awkward conversation for me. For Roger? Not so much. In fact, he loved that conversation.) After that he was very liberal with the compliments about my chest, my eyes, my rear.

It definitely made getting undressed in front of him easier, and eventually, fun.

The Confidence Issue

When Erin and I started writing this book, our first step was to find out what women are thinking about sex. So we put together a list of women we know—women of all ages and all walks of life—and asked them the good, the bad, and the ugly about sex. And as we read their answers, one thing became abundantly clear early on: women have a confidence issue.

Here are just a few of the responses we read:

> I want to have a great sex life with my husband, but every time we start to have sex, little voices pop into my head telling me I'm not pretty enough, thin enough, good enough to please my husband. And my desire comes screeching to a halt.

> When I have sex, I worry the whole time about how I look and how I'm performing. I can hardly enjoy it because the worry takes over and my focus goes from him to me.

> I'm not a sex kitten and I'm certainly not a Victoria's Secret model. And while I know my husband doesn't expect me to be, there's some part of me that looks in the mirror and starts to compare. Even worse, I start to wonder if my husband is comparing too. It's an intimacy killer for sure.

Have you ever felt like that? I have! I can't even begin to tell you how many times I've walked down that negative self-talk trail. It often starts with the best intentions. I see Roger and I want to be intimate with him. I want to show him how much I love him. I want to have sex with him. But then that little voice starts talking. I'm having a bad hair day. I need to lose another ten pounds. I'm not nearly as graceful or svelte as a runway model. And suddenly, what should be an intimate, marriage-building time turns into just the opposite.

How do we stop that?

How do we learn to be confident as the women God created us to be so we can be what our husbands need from us? And how can we stop the negative self-talk so that we can enjoy intimacy without constantly worrying about our performance?

We Can Talk Honestly with Our Husbands

When I'm running through the world, looking at other women with impossibly tight bodies on TV or seeing women on the street who have it all together, I can get into the mindset of, *Of course he's not interested in me. How could he be?* But when I actually talk to Roger about sex, I am reminded that he is very much into me, and do you think there is a hotel nearby that we could duck into?

One of the best things I've done for my sex life is to tell Roger about my lack of confidence so he can quickly counteract it. My "Hey, hon, I'm feeling a bit self-conscious about my arm flab" is often met with "What arm flab?" He's a smart man. I've found that the more my husband and I talk about sex, the more I understand that he really is into me—and the more I'm able to push aside those silly thoughts about arm flab and focus on intimacy with him.

We Can Choose to Not Allow Negative Thoughts

My friend M became a Christian about a year ago. She said God completely transformed her, but she still had some bad habits to break and one of them was swearing. So she started to wear a pink rubber bracelet and every time she catches herself swearing, she switches it to the other wrist. If she gets to the end of the day and the bracelet hasn't been moved, she rewards herself with a dollar toward a good book.

I think I need to do that too.

Not for the swearing, but for the negative self-talk. Every time I think something bad about myself—that my belly is flabby or my legs are too short or that Roger won't want me—I'm going to trade the bracelet. And if I can get through a day without degrading myself in my mind, then I'm going to put a dollar into an envelope to save up for some snazzy new lingerie. Anyone want to join me?

Because we have to stop degrading ourselves.

And start loving ourselves for who we really are.

We Can Intentionally Focus on the Positive

You are beautiful.

And not just on the inside.

In fact, just to prove it to yourself, I want you to think of five of your physical characteristics that you know are great assets. Do you have great hair? Gorgeous eyes? Long legs? Tight buns? Whatever it is, I want you to think about those things when you're having sex. Instead of *What if he sees my back fat?* think *I need to turn this way so he can see my rock-hard calves.* If your mind is too busy focusing on your positive qualities, it will all but forget about that leftover baby weight.

We Can Practice Often

I don't have any scientific research to quote here, but I do have considerable personal experience. And this is how it goes in my marriage: the longer it's been since we've had sex, the more my husband wants it. (And the grumpier he is, but that's another chapter.) The longer it's been since we've had sex, the less I want it. I don't really understand the chemistry behind that, but that's how I feel.

I think it's all about the mental "gearing up" that has to take place for us girls to get into it. It takes time. But there is a touchy-feely time after sex when we are still in the "sex bubble" and we remember what it felt like very vividly. And that memory drives glances across the room, a little extra touching, and the knowledge that none of our teens knew that we were getting it on upstairs while they were making a grilled cheese downstairs. Which, of course, drives more getting it on.

So my advice if you're struggling with confidence while you're having sex is to have more sex. Because the more you have, the more you will want. And the more you want, the more you will flirt. And the more you flirt, the more you will get. And the more you get, the more confidence you will have that your husband wants you. Makes sense, right? (By the way, if you do want to see scientific research on this, the blogs www.sexwithinmarriage.com and www.themarriagebed.com have done loads of surveys that will lend a lot of insight into these sorts of things.)

We Can Remember We Are Worth the Wait

One of the biggest confidence boosts I've had is understanding that I'm worth waiting for. Sometimes I don't feel like having sex, but I know it's important to my man. Most of the time I suck it up and do it, and eventually, I get in the mood as well. But yes, there have been a couple of times I've said, "Could we make a date for tomorrow night? I'm exhausted." Roger has never refused, and I'm always grateful that we both work hard to put each other's needs above our own. And I have to say, knowing he's willing to wait for me makes me feel like a wanted woman.

We Can Believe Our Husbands When They Say We Are Hot

You know all that negative self-talk you have? Your husband never thinks any of these things—and I can prove it. Jay Dee at www.sexwithinmarriage.com did a survey asking men if they found their wives attractive, and over 95 percent of men answered an exuberant yes to that question.[1] But even more interesting is this: 81 percent of those respondents said that their wives were more attractive (or at least as attractive) now than they were on the day they got married. Yep, your man thinks you're getting hotter as you age. (For the record: the same survey found that 76 percent of husbands wanted to have more sex and 71 percent of husbands felt like their wife had a confidence issue when it came to sex. Interesting, right?)

My point here? When your husband says you're looking hot, he means it. And not only does he think you're hot, he thinks you're hotter than you were on your wedding day. And that was before your boobs got saggy. So believe him. And then show him the hot mama that you are.

A *Hot Mama* PLEDGE

I know that confidence will bring more enjoyment to my sex life, so I will

- work to grow my confidence in my own body, so that I can fully give myself to my husband.

- have open and honest conversations with my husband about my body issues so that we can work together to help me get over them.

- set aside negative self-talk about my body so that I can fully enjoy sex in the way God intended.

REAL *Hot Mama* IDEAS

"I decided to keep track of all the times I had a bad thought about my body for a day. So I opened up a little note on my iPhone and just wrote a quick 'p' (it's the key closest to my thumb on the keypad) every time I thought something about my weight, my body type, my arm fat. At the end of the day, I had 47 'p's.' How sad is that? I made a promise to myself that I'm going to work on whittling down that number—and every time I think one bad thought, I have to think five positive ones. I'm not fully there yet, but I'll break this habit once and for all."—B

"I initiated sex . . . with the lights on. This is totally crazy, but in our ten-year marriage, I have never initiated sex. And not because I didn't want to, but because every time I started to think about it, I got fearful that he may not want me. Or that he'd think I wasn't pretty enough. After reading this chapter, I told myself that I had to stop, so I made myself initiate sex that night. He was shocked—but good shocked. And I'm already thinking about when I'm going to do it again."—U

"I asked my husband what he likes about how I look and his list was really long. He just kept going and going and going. Smart man. He'll be getting some tonight."—N

Hot Mama
"Confidence Is Key" BUCKET LIST

1. Leave the lights on when you have sex. I promise (cross my heart!) that your husband *will* be thinking about how you look—and he'll be thinking you look hot.

2. Write a list of all of your body insecurities. Burn it. Then write a list of all of the parts of your body you think look great and tack it to your bathroom mirror.

3. Head to our Facebook page (www.facebook.com/hotmama guides) and sign up for a free Hot Mama Consultation with one of our stylist friends. Get some confidence-building fashion ideas tailored just for you.

4. Check out one (or ten) of our fashion challenges from our ebook *10 Quick Fashion Fixes to Feel Confident and Sexy: A Hot Mama Challenge.* (Warning, these challenges are proven to make a mama feel red hot.)

5. Wear lingerie. Tonight.

6. Ask your husband what he likes about your body. Take notes. Then make sure to show him all those parts often in the next week.

7. Find a way—whether it's a bracelet or accountability with a friend—to stop the negative self-talk.

4

Throw Out the Guilt

For as high as the heavens are above the earth,
    so great is his steadfast love toward those who
      fear him;
as far as the east is from the west,
    so far does he remove our transgressions from
      us.

                            Psalm 103:11–12 ESV

(Erin)

My husband and I were asked to be sex counselors.

Actually, we were just asked to meet and chat with K and B, a couple in our Sunday school class who were about to get married. This was back in 2002, and since Cameron and I had a whopping two years of marital experience, we were the obvious choice. Ha. Truth was, we were young and naïve and had struggled for all of our two years, and I think the

Sunday school leaders knew that we would be real and raw and honest.

Which it turns out K and B didn't need.

What they needed was some grace.

We invited K and B over for dinner. When they arrived, I set out a lovely cheese plate on my wedding china (that may have been the first time I used it) and I poured iced tea and we headed to the living room to talk. We chatted about their wedding plans and their honeymoon and all of the basic wedding stuff and then I dropped the bomb: "So, what are you most scared about?"

It seemed like an innocent enough question to ask. It wasn't.

B looked at K and then back at us. She opened her mouth and then shut it again. She bit her lip. And then she burst out: "Sex."

"Sex?" Cameron asked. He was incredulous.

"Yeah. Sex."

"What do you mean?"

K took over. "We uh . . . we uh . . . we've already had sex. So I guess that means we'll never be blessed with a great sex life, right?"

Gulp.

A lot of people feel like K and B.

As Christians we walk a fine line. God calls us to live a life that's honoring to him. His statutes aren't around to give us a bunch of rules, but instead to help us to live the best, most joyful lives that we can. Sex outside of marriage breaks that standard. It may be temporarily fun, but God knows that in the long term, it's not best for our bodies, emotions, or souls.

We serve a God of grace. When we turn to him and repent he forgives us no matter what. He's not vindictive and he doesn't hold a grudge. He's not going to punish us for our past sins. Which means that people like K and B need only to turn to him and away from their sin, and he will restore them. Like new. And while natural consequences may ensue, God never withholds restoration. Or hope.

We are new in Christ. And no matter what you have done sexually in the past, God can and will restore you. Yet so many Christians live their lives mired in guilt and shame— they assume that because they experimented sexually outside of marriage that their sex life is forever doomed. It's not. That is a lie that will rob you of the pleasure and hope that comes from truly being a forgiven and cherished child of God.

And it will rob you of the intimate, close, and beautiful sexual relationship that God intended for you and your spouse.

It's time to let go of the guilt—whatever you did sexually before today needs to be handed to God right now. Forgiven, forgotten, and put in the past.

And instead, you need to look toward the future that God has intended for you all along.

Living without Guilt

It's rough being a girl.

We have to be everything for everyone. The best moms to our kids. The best employees for our employers. The best chefs for our families. The best housekeepers for our houses. And, the hottest, sexiest wives in existence for our husbands.

And if we fail at any of these things, we feel guilty.

We have to just stop.

I have a feeling I'm going to be telling you to stop a lot while writing this book, but it's true. As women, we have to stop. There is no room in our lives for guilt—not when we serve such a loving, forgiving, hopeful God. He just doesn't want us muddled down by guilt (or any of the other stuff we muddle ourselves down with) when he wants so much joy for us.

But many of us have been feeling guilty about sex for a long time, for a lot of reasons. And that deep-seated guilt is affecting our sex lives in a bad way. It puts us in the mindset of "we can't." Instead, let's explore some "we can" truths to make our own, to help us develop new patterns of thinking.

We Can Trust in God's Redemption

My friend L got a bottle of white wine and a pack of condoms for her fourteenth birthday, along with a note from her mom telling her to go out and have fun. By the time she turned twenty, she couldn't remember how many sex partners she'd had.

Then she met F. He was a Christian, and over a series of several years he not only led her to Christ but he made her his bride. And while he forgave her past fully and completely, L had a really hard time forgiving herself.

She felt guilty because she was worried her previous sexual experiences made her husband think she was dirty or unclean. And she worried that her sex life would never be strong or intimate because she had "given away the milk" for so long (her words, not mine).

But God redeemed L.

It took many months of work with a counselor and some close, accountable friends, but eventually L was able to not only give her past to God, but trust that God had redeemed her. The past was in the past.

And now she walks forward cleanly. And without the shame and guilt that blinded her for so long.

We Can Bring Guilt into the Light

Whatever is in your sexual past, let me reassure you: you are forgiven. God has forgotten. And your husband still loves you. But I'm realizing that many women still doubt those truths even while accepting that God is a God of grace.

We interviewed many, many hot mamas for this book, and after poring over their thoughts and feelings about sex, I started to notice a common thread. Many of the women who felt shackled by guilt also felt embarrassed to share about their guilt. One woman told me she was afraid for her husband to know she had feelings of guilt about sex because he might think she was being dramatic and seeking trouble where there was no trouble to be had. Another woman revealed that she hadn't fully told her husband about her sexual past for fear that he might find her dirty or undesirable.

Guilt and shame thrive in the dark. The more they are stuffed away, hidden, or kept out of the light, the more they will poison your soul. Don't let that happen! Talk to your husband. Tell him what you're thinking and feeling. And bring that guilt and shame right into the light, where it will fade away and be replaced by emotional intimacy and trust.

Of course, if you're anything like me, those tough conversations don't just happen. I remember a day a few weeks ago when I knew I needed to have a tough talk with my husband. He walked down the stairs after the kids went to bed and suddenly my throat felt tight. It was as if the words just got stuck in my throat and I couldn't bring myself to say them. I actually stalled so much that the conversation didn't happen for several days . . . several days that I spent worrying and feeling guilty. I should have just told him to begin with.

My friend M told me, "I don't think I've really had a good conversation about my upbringing and sex with my husband. Which is odd, because I feel we are very open in most areas and hello, he likes to discuss sex." For some reason, sexual guilt often seems off-limits with couples. But it's a necessary conversation and I encourage you to have it.

We Can Check Guilt at the Bedroom Door

I have a rule in my house that my kids have to check complaining at the kitchen door. So there's this spot on the wall right by the door—it's covered in smudged fingerprints now—that my kids hit as they walk in to symbolize that the house is a no-complaint zone. (Lest you want to hire me as supernanny, I want to clarify that my kids still complain in the house. But I choose to believe that our little symbolic "door check" at least minimizes it.)

Anyway, guilt has something in common with complaining. It's a choice. And we can choose to set it aside so we can enjoy time with our husbands guilt-free. So next time you walk into your bedroom, I want you to tap the doorframe (or slap it if you want), symbolizing that your guilt about sex is staying outside of the room. And then go inside and enjoy yourself without allowing yourself to think about all those things.

We Can Know the Difference between Truth and Lies

Guilt is a lie.

And if you really consider the reasons you're feeling guilty or ashamed, you will probably start to see that. My sister Alisa says that when she starts feeling ashamed or guilty about an area in her life, she opens her journal and draws a line down the middle. On one side, she writes "what I'm feeling" and on the other she writes "what is true." Then she fills in the columns. So, for example, this is a recent page from her journal:

What I'm Feeling	What Is True
Guilty that I left the kids with a babysitter so I could go out on a date night with my husband.	God made our marriages our most important human relationships and we have to put them as a priority over anything else.
Guilty that I can't seem to manage my life as a mom without feeling like I'm having a breakdown, which leads me to be cranky and impatient.	I have three very young kids, I'm pregnant, and I'm really tired. In order to be the best wife and mom I can be, I need to take care of myself.

Isn't that cool? I think by simply comparing how you're feeling to what you know is true, you will find that most of the guilt and shame you feel isn't based in truth. And when you know it's not true, it will be much easier to set it aside and not let it steal your joy. Or your intimacy.

We Can Pursue Redemption

My friend M has a very interesting past when it comes to sex. (Don't worry, she told me I could share it with you.) She grew up in a very religious home where sex wasn't talked about. Sadly, her first experience with sex was abusive. She was only sixteen. And because of the feelings of guilt and shame surrounding that situation, she stayed silent about the abuse. She said she made it acceptable in her own mind by deciding to have sex on her own terms, by making it her choice.

Reflecting on it now, she says she didn't even have the wherewithal to understand what true intimacy was, or that the false intimacy she was seeking was so damaging. No one ever taught her about sex as an intimate act. Instead, she learned from the media and from her peers.

So for years she allowed men to use her, convincing herself that sex was meaningless to her. That the only thing she had to give was her body. Many years later, she got married and became a Christian. She knew sex was something she needed to give her husband and so she did—coldly and without emotion. She said she forced herself to have sex with her husband again and again without ever enjoying it, convincing herself that she had lost that possibility long ago.

Her husband—a man who loved God and loved her—saw it differently. He encouraged her to go to counseling to redeem that area of her life, and she agreed to try. In counseling, the therapist told her that the only reason she should be having sex is for intimacy and enjoyment. He said she needed to look at it as simply a way for her to enjoy her husband and for him to enjoy her.

M laughed.

She told the therapist that if that were the case, she would never have sex again because she was certain she would never, ever enjoy it. She was willing to do it for her husband whom she loved, but she would never enjoy it. And never see it as anything more than a chore.

The counselor asked her to pray for redemption.

With the counselor's help, she realized that intimacy as God designed it, at its core, is the most perfect physical manifestation of the bride of Christ. She learned to accept Christ's unconditional, redemptive love and to find new life—not only through redemption from her sins but also through the redemption of intimacy in her marriage.

M says that God delivered her from her past and redeemed her sex life. It wasn't overnight, but in time M found herself desiring her husband. She says she now understands that sex is supposed to be a beautiful picture of the giving and receiving of unconditional love, like in our relationship with Christ. By acknowledging that the sex she'd had in the past was not at all the way God intended it, she was able to heal and forgive and begin trying to understand what God's true design for sex was. And it became beautiful instead of the constant Achilles' heel in her marriage.

Like M, you may have some past guilt and shame that are standing in the way of your intimacy. If you're feeling overwhelmed by feelings of guilt or shame—no matter where they are coming from or what they are about—I suggest you seek the help of a professional Christian counselor or a pastor. Even a few sessions can help you to uncover the truth behind your guilt and start walking forward. You are worth it.

And so is your marriage.

A *Hot Mama* PLEDGE

I am a redeemed daughter of God and my sins have been forgiven, so I will

- confess my transgressions and ask for forgiveness—and then stop thinking about them.

- have a conversation with my husband about how guilt has affected my perspective on sex and then work together to get over it.

- allow the past to be in the past and let hot mama sex be my present.

REAL *Hot Mama* IDEAS

"I tried the journal thing Erin's sister talked about. On the left side, I wrote about how worried I am that I lost all chances of ever having a good sex life because we had sex before we were married. Then, I started praying about the right side and realized what was true: God is not vindictive. We made a mistake but he has forgiven us and washed us clean. And now because we have both repented, he can and will bless us with a beautiful sex life. It was very reassuring."—L

"I made an appointment with a counselor. I know it seems like a simple step, but it was a big one for me. I'm anxious to start healing."—D

"I grew up in a very conservative home and church environment where sexuality was either not discussed or was not discussed as something that was positive/permissible, especially for girls. I think that message is very hard to just switch off once you are married and 'allowed' to be sexual. It's something I've struggled with. And one of the hardest things for me was to just have a conversation with my husband about it. I had no idea how to bring it up or what to even say, but one night, I just let it all out. It was a teary, blubbery mess, but he took me into his arms and listened to me. And now I feel so much closer to him. And I truly want to have sex with him because I know it's good for me. And for us."—N

Hot Mama
"Throw Out the Guilt" BUCKET LIST

1. On your own, pray and confess any past sexual sin that you have. Ask God to forgive you and help you to forget. Then spend some time praying with a trusted friend or accountability partner about any residual guilt you feel. Confess your past sin to them and pray together that God will bring a release from guilt and help you live into the forgiveness that is already yours.

2. Buy a couple's devotional (try *Draw Close* by Willard and Joyce Harley) and read it every night with your husband. Intentionally focus on discussing those things that make you feel guilty or ashamed and bringing them into the light.

3. Spend some time reading all of the Bible verses about sex and sexual intimacy. (Look up the words *sex*, *marriage*, and *intimacy* in your Bible's concordance, and it will give you a list of verses.) This will not only give you some perspective on why God created sex, but will also help you to seek God's design for sex rather than the world's or your own. Start by reading Ephesians 5, 1 Corinthians 13, and the entire book of Song of Solomon.

4. Talk to your husband about your guilt. Just tell him what you're feeling and allow him to reassure you.

47

5

Hot Dates over Playdates

You make known to me the path of life;
    you will fill me with joy in your presence,
    with eternal pleasures at your right hand.
                                    Psalm 16:11

(Kathi)

Sex and kids are not compatible.

Actually, I take that back. Sex is great for making kids, but kids are not great for making sex. It's ironic, really, seeing that's how most of us got the little blessings in the first place, but any parent of a kid under twenty-seven will tell you the same thing I'm telling you: kids make sex almost impossible.

Notice I said *almost* impossible.

Not completely impossible.

And I'm here to tell you today that with some effort, careful planning, and extraordinary feats of hot mama-ness, you can have an amazing sex life and have kids too. In fact, the reason that we called this book *Hot Mama* (and not, say, *Hot Young Twenties Woman without Anything to Hold Her Back*) is because we think moms actually have the potential to have the hottest sex lives.

They just have to work at it.

Just because something is challenging doesn't mean we should stop trying. (Except—apparently for me—going to the gym on a regular basis.) Sex is important. And you have to make it a priority, difficult or not. That's what this chapter is about. Helping you to say no to another PTA meeting (I didn't have to ask you twice, did I?) and yes to more hot mama time with your husband. Helping you to scoot that pile of laundry off the bed so you have more room to, well, you know.

Because kids may not be conducive to sex, but hot mamas certainly are.

And I'm here to tell you exactly how to get there in all of your hot mama glory.

When Roger and I got married, I thought we had it so much easier than most parents. Since we were a blended family, we had no babies in our brood—in fact, our youngest was thirteen. We could go to the movies or out to dinner anytime our schedules allowed. Plus, we had big kids who did things like leave the house without being strapped into the minivan and had a basic understanding that a locked door probably meant that we didn't want them to bang on it until we opened it.

I thought we had it made.

Sadly, I was wrong. It wasn't *our* schedules that got in the way, it was the schedules of our kids. There was always a practice that they needed to be at or a job they needed a ride to. Our evenings were crowded with tons of activities and our weekends were just as busy. We were to-do-listing ourselves out of sex.

We needed a different plan.

As I said before, sex and kids just aren't compatible. And if you have kids—whether they are two or twenty—sex just isn't going to happen unless you plan for it. And make it a priority. And realize that all those little to-dos that creep into your life are getting in the way of your most important to-do: your husband.

You are a creative woman. I know this because I've seen the garlands you made out of egg cartons on Pinterest. And those egg carton garlands are amazing—don't get me wrong—but what if you were to put the same energy into something that will make your husband and you much happier at the end of the day?

I want you to get really creative about sex. No, we're not talking the latest *Cosmopolitan* trick that will "drive your man wild." (Really, how many more "new" positions could there be without displacing a hip?) No, we want you to get creative with time and location: the when and the where of sex. Roger and I have had to be super-creative in this area, and we pass our wisdom on to you. Here are some parent-friendly ideas to help you and your hubby.

Finding Time for Sex in a Jam-Packed Schedule

You know those crazy weeks when you can't even find a fifteen-minute window in your calendar to take a shower? Yeah. We all have those. I remember a week a few months ago when I was on a book deadline. On top of that, I had scheduled speaking engagements at two different MOPS groups—one in Northern California and one in Southern California. Additionally, we had planned a big old family brunch at our house.

Let's just say that I felt a bit frantic.

And the idea of penciling in sex on top of all that? Completely daunting.

But—and there always is a *but*—I scheduled it anyway. Not because I felt like I had time or that I even had energy, but because I knew it had to be my priority. I may have done it grudgingly (the first time) but you know what? It was so worth it. Because when I put a little effort into Roger—and felt that intimacy and support that only come from being with the man I love—I was suddenly emotionally energized. I felt like I could conquer the whole world.

I want you to have that same feeling on those days when you feel like you're drowning in a sea of to-dos and need all the support you can get. So here are some easy, schedule-conducive ways to have your sex and your schedule too:

- **The shower.** Taking a quick shower together is something you can do at home, even when the kids are there.
- **Loud TV.** Experts will tell you that a TV in the bedroom is the killer of romance. I disagree. A loud TV is what saved our sex life when Roger and I had teens in the house.
- **Early in the morning or late at night.** If you're both early birds, morning sex can be a great way to start your day. Set your alarm early and squeeze in some alone time

before the kids get up. Or if you're night owls, get into bed early and tire yourselves out.

- **Nooner.** While the kids are in school. 'Nuff said.

Getting Smart about Childcare

But wait! you're probably thinking. *I'd love to have sex every morning and every night. But there's this thing called kids. And my kids wake up at 4:37 a.m. And they need a glass of water at 11:27 p.m. And they seem to need me for large portions of the day to boot.*

Roger and I were lucky to have only teenagers when we got married. But I am aware that many of you have young kids. Kids who are unable to entertain themselves while you take a quick hop in the sack. When your kids are young, that's when you have to be extra, super-duper creative. Here are a few tricks:

- **Have a regular drop-off babysitter.** Finding a babysitter takes time and effort. (And we've already established, you don't have time for sex, much less time to find a babysitter so you can have sex.) The trick to eliminating babysitter-search time is to make your babysitter a regular thing. My friend U scheduled her babysitter to watch her kids every Tuesday night as a standing thing—that way, she has no excuse not to make time for her husband. Even better, she asked if she could drop her kids off at her babysitter's house—that way, she and her husband don't have to spend loads of money on dinner out every week—and they have the house to themselves.

- **Camp Grandma.** Erin's mom has Camp Grandma every Wednesday night. She orders pizza or makes a huge pot of mac & cheese, has a movie and pillows out, and usually makes homemade chocolate chip cookies. Any of her eleven grandkids can show up anytime between five thirty and nine and be guaranteed dinner, fun, and cousin time. That means Erin and her siblings have a standing date night every week. And yes, there is a line of people waiting to be adopted into the family. I asked.

- **Schedule playdates.** For the kids, not you. Ask a friend to swap afternoon playdates—you take her kids for one Saturday afternoon and then she takes yours the next. But, lest I've been unclear, these are not the times for catching up on errands.

- **Sleepovers.** When your kids are having a sleepover, have your own. Plan for sex and then go out the next morning for a long, leisurely breakfast. Keep giving each other knowing glances that mean you got some last night (and maybe again in the morning).

- **Event sex.** Roger and I always took one day a year to go Christmas shopping. It was a day off of work, so as soon as the kids were off to school, we'd crawl back into bed and have sex, then get ready for our day of shopping. Bonus: Roger was in a much better shopping mood once he had sex. Yes, that was only once a year, but we looked forward to it starting in October!

- **When all else fails, put a special movie on.** You just know that a lot of parents were having extra cuddle time when *Frozen* finally became available for download.

(Because you know kids everywhere Did. Not. Move. for 102 minutes of frozen fun.)

Get in the Mood

Of course, even when the stars align and you have (a) child-care and (b) time and (c) a good hair day simultaneously, there's still one more factor: the mood. It's hard to get in the mood for sex. Especially when you've spent your day explaining why Barney really isn't a real dinosaur and why frogs really don't belong in bedrooms. You're exhausted. You're worn out. And really, what sounds awfully nice is a nice long bath and a relaxing foot rub.

As a mom, you don't have long, leisurely amounts of time for sex. So when you do have time, you need to get yourself in the mood. And fast. Here are a few of my ideas:

- **Take a shower.** Take a warm shower, get nice and squeaky clean, and think about your husband. How amazing he is. How much he does to provide for your family. What a great dad he is. How hot he is . . .
- **Dress the part.** This would be a good time to put on some lingerie (or if the kids are in the house, slip on a hot mama pair of panties under your jeans).
- **Plan a chore list.** I let Roger know early in our marriage that, mentally, something about him helping around the house got me ready for sex. No, it wasn't, "Wow baby, you're so sexy when you scrub those toilets . . ." But I knew that when we were working together toward a common goal (say, getting the kitchen clean or sprucing

up the back patio), I did feel closer to him. And when we stated early on, "Hey, let's get the chores done and then we can head upstairs," there was a lot more touchy-feely going on during chore time.

- **Just do it.** Just start kissing your man. I can almost promise that within a few minutes, you'll be in the mood.

Work on Your Logistics

For Roger and me, our hot dates often took place at noon.

At least once a week, and sometimes more often than that, Roger and I met up for lunch. We both worked and both had schedules to keep, but we could always both take a lunch break. Those dates became our lifeline. We would look forward to those times together—without chores or kids—as a little getaway from real life. We would laugh, talk, and sometimes even pull out our calendars. (Getting caught up on schedules is a very marriage-saving activity.) But most of the time we were just on a date, loving and listening. Oh, and occasionally we'd head home for a little something before heading back to work.

When you're in a marriage, you do have schedules to keep and kids to pick up. So in order to make sex a priority, you have to figure out all those logistics and make it work. Whatever it takes. It's kind of like a puzzle—let's squeeze sex in here while the kids are at soccer and then steal a few kisses here while they're distracted with the football game. Here are a few logistics that worked for us:

- **Everyone—out!** It's okay to kick everyone out, well, as long as they are old enough to leave on their own. Let them all know that Friday night you need the house to yourselves from five to nine. I promise you, your kids will not be traumatized. (Okay, maybe for a bit, but they will recover. Promise.)

- **Business trips.** In our relationship, I'm the one who has the most out-of-town business trips. But whenever I go someplace fun, I make sure to take Roger along. Nice hotels, great food, fun people. What could be better for a marriage?

- **A bedroom door lock.** I am amazed at how many couples don't have a lock on their bedroom door. In our house, a locked door means that mom and dad are having alone time. Sometimes alone time means sex, sometimes it means a massage, and sometimes it means the sexiest thing in the world—a nap. But "don't come in" is the chief message in a locked door. Teach your kids from an early age to follow that rule and sneak off to do their own very quiet thing without interrupting.

A *Hot Mama* PLEDGE

I want sex to be a top priority in my life, so I will

- put sex above the other to-dos in my life—even above laundry and playdates.

- allow myself to make sex one of the most important parts of my to-do list instead of something that gets pushed aside.

- get creative with my schedule so that I have time and energy for sex.

REAL *Hot Mama* IDEAS

"We usually put our daughter down for a nap around nine and I often exercise while she's taking a nap. However, this time, instead of cuing the workout DVD, I changed into lingerie and surprised him with a 'different workout.' He was definitely surprised and we both enjoyed it. It was nice to do something spontaneous when so much of my life is wrapped around my baby's schedule."—T

"I did it. I booked a weekend away for us at a bed and breakfast. I've never done anything like this before—for some reason, I always make excuses that we don't have time or we don't have money. But that's just not true. We don't make time and we don't find room in our budget for us. That has to change. When my husband got home, I told him what I had done and he looked at me wide-eyed. Then he broke into the biggest grin and pulled me into his arms. I think he's excited too."—U

"My husband and I both work during the day outside of our home, and when we get home from work, our lives are a whir of dinner making, lunch packing, clothes washing, and planning for the next day. But today, I sent him texts sporadically throughout the work day: the first one when I pulled out of the driveway for work, the next during my lunch break, a couple when I was running errands after work. I even sent him one in the evening while our son was still awake. Let's just say that our bedtime routine was very short that evening."—T

Hot Mama

"Hot Dates over Playdates" BUCKET LIST

1. Look at your schedule for the week and find four creative times when you can have sex. Make it happen.

2. Call a friend and see if you can trade playdates sometime this week. Spend your playdate time naked.

3. Wake your husband up with sex first thing in the morning.

4. Tell your husband you are going to have sex every day this week (or month, if you are brave!). Find a time to do it every day even if your schedules are jam-packed.

5. Take a shower together while you're getting ready for the day.

6. Plan a sex event for one day in the future—maybe an overnighter while the kids go to Grandma's or going on a road trip to a bed and breakfast next fall. Whatever it is, make sure that sex is your main focus.

7. Pounce on your husband as soon as the kids fall asleep for some pre–TV time sex.

6

Getting over Our Good Girl Issues

Enjoy life with your wife, whom you love, all the days of this meaningless life that God has given you under the sun—all your meaningless days.

Ecclesiastes 9:9

(Erin)

Good girls don't like sex. Right? Right?!

I grew up as a card-carrying member of the First Baptist Church Valedictorian's Club (a group in which, strangely, I was the only member). Because of this, I was never going to think about sex, talk about sex, consider sex, or get myself into a situation where I may be tempted to have sex.

Because I was (obviously) a good girl. And I had a purity ring, a purity necklace, and a purity notebook where I carefully recorded purity-related revelations to prove it. I had no intention of ever changing my attitude toward sex. Ever.

I got a little older. I started dating guys. I held hands. I stole a few kisses on my parents' front porch. I even had a few serious relationships that lasted months. And through it all, I held to my belief: Sex is bad. Good girls don't think about sex, talk about sex, or have sex.

Then I got married.

And strangely, even though it was finally okay to do the one thing I had avoided for so long, it felt weird. I had a hard time flipping the switch and changing my mindset from "Good girls don't have sex" to "Good wives not only have sex, they like it." It was a big shift to make—especially to make in one day.

Time passed.

I talked to friends. I talked to counselors. I got more used to the idea that sex is okay. And I began to accept that sex was part of my marriage and even that it was an important part of building intimacy in my marriage. And so I did it.

But I rarely enjoyed it. I wouldn't let myself. Because I allowed myself to believe a lie: women don't like sex.

But here's the thing: I know that most of us girls actually like sex when we get down to it. My hot mama friends made it very clear to me as I wrote this chapter that girls *do* like sex. But they also made something else clear: when push comes to shove and babies start demanding attention, it's easy to start living like sex is a chore. Or a "man's thing." It's not.

Girls, sex is awesome.

It's not an annoyance. It's not something we do only to make our husbands happy. It's something we do to make our marriages stronger. And—here's the kicker—it's something we do to make ourselves happy.

God made sex for both men and women. And he made it to be something both men and women enjoy. As women, we should be grabbing our husbands and kissing them breathless. And then taking them to bed.

No excuses. No headaches. No false assumptions.

Ladies, can we just make a vow to each other right now to stop acting like sex is only for our men? Like it's just something we have to tolerate? Of course, there will be days when we're tired or angry or emotional or run-down. And on those days, it's fine to take a break. (We'll talk more about that in the next chapter.) But having an off day doesn't have to mean that you don't enjoy sex. God made sex for us. He wants us to enjoy it. And I'm not about to let a so-called headache stand in the way.

God Created Sex for Connection

Sex is the ultimate connecting tool.

Having sex is the one thing you do only with your husband that will make you feel close, connected, and totally in tune with him physically, emotionally, and spiritually.

God knew married folks needed to connect on a level that went way beyond other human relationships. And he knew that only through this deep, heartfelt, and truly intimate act would couples truly join together as one.

It wasn't made for men. It wasn't made for women. It was made for both of you. And for your marriage. And because of this, you have a job to do: release all of that hot mama vixen that's cooped up inside of you.

God Created Sex for Enjoyment

Most girls have been taught that sex is for boys from the time they started being taught about sex. I already confessed that I grew up thinking of sex as dirty—a result of my conservative upbringing. What I haven't mentioned is that I also entered my marriage thinking sex was for boys to enjoy and for girls to, well, tolerate.

How sad.

And how completely different from how God intended sex to be. Just in case you didn't catch on earlier in this book when I was having you read about sex in the Bible, let me make it *über* clear: God made sex to be enjoyed. By both the man and the woman. God wants you to have your cake and eat it too and not feel guilty even a little bit because he wanted you to eat the whole slice.

Isn't that freeing?

And also a little bit fun?

I know the realization was freeing to me—because I had spent too much time worrying about how I *should* feel and too little focusing on how I did feel. And those shoulds were standing in the way of my fun. (And, in case you didn't already know this, sex is fun.)

You Are Beautifully and Wonderfully Made

You were made to have sex with your husband. Beautifully. Wonderfully. And intimately.

I'm not saying you are capable of any and every position. But I am saying that God made you with the full capacity to please your husband.

And made him to please you.

I say this because as we outlined in chapter 3, confidence stands in the way of many women fully enjoying sex. And I'm starting to realize that often "I have a headache" actually means "I have a confidence issue."

A few nights ago, my husband rolled over and started rubbing my back. He has this lotion that smells like lavender and vanilla and I closed my eyes and . . . well, long story short, we didn't have sex.

I wanted to, for a minute.

But then my confidence—or lack thereof—stood in the way. I started thinking about how sore I was from going to the gym the day before. Which made me think about the fact that I haven't been very good about going to the gym lately (hence the soreness). Which made me start worrying about belly flab. Which made me feel like if we had sex, maybe my husband would notice said belly flab and not want me anymore.

Totally ridiculous, right?

But I think that often our insecurities about our bodies, coupled with fear of performance, stand in the way of us enjoying sex. Which is so sad, because the reality is so obvious: our husbands want us. Belly flab, sore muscles, lack of flexibility, and all.

So next time you find yourself spinning down that path into I'm-not-good-enough land, stop yourself right there. And then roll over and show your husband exactly what you can do in bed.

Trust me. You are enough.

You Can Initiate Sex Sometimes

While we were writing the ebook *10 Ideas to Inspire Red Hot Sex*, I challenged many of my friends to initiate sex with their husbands in a fun and creative way and give me feedback on it. (Yes, it was a little awkward, but my friends all thanked me later—one of the perils of being friends with an author.)

My friend B wrote me a note and said, "Wow! I realized after doing your challenge that I have fallen into the habit of letting my husband always initiate sex. He's good at initiating and he does it often so we just sort of fell into a routine where I waited for him to take charge."

B decided to change that. One night, she took charge and initiated sex, and her husband was not only ecstatic, he thanked her the next day. And made pancakes for breakfast. She told me later that she realizes that when she initiates sex, it makes her husband "goofy happy—because he knows he is wanted and desired."

By simply initiating sex, B helped her husband feel desired, wanted, and joyful.

I read B's words and they hit me like a ton of bricks.

Because I do the same thing to my husband. It's not that I don't like to have sex with him or even that I don't desire him, but simply that it's easier to just wait for him to initiate. And I realized that by waiting for him to initiate, I was telling him that I didn't desire him as much as he desired me.

Not true.

I remedied that very quickly.

At bedtime, after we read books and do prayers with our kids, I usually head downstairs to catch up from the day while Cameron stays upstairs and tucks them each into bed.

A few nights ago, instead of heading downstairs to load the dishwasher, I headed downstairs and changed into a cute little nightie. I pulled back the covers of the bed, lit some candles, and waited for him to come down.

He was also goofy happy.

In fact, when I suggested he make pancakes the next morning, he happily obliged.

Realize That Every Relationship Is Different

My friend N told me that when they were in premarital counseling, the pastor asked her husband how many times a week was the "right amount of times" to have sex. His answer was nine. N said she spit out her water.

I asked Cameron that same question a few minutes ago and he told me three—which is probably about the same as my answer. (Look at us on the same page and all.)

But not every relationship is the same.

And my friend S told me that she has always been the one in her relationship with the higher sex drive. She told me that "in the early years of our marriage, him saying no to sex devastated me. I wondered if I wasn't pretty enough. Or if I didn't turn him on. I've learned now (after eight years) that he is just not interested as often as I am. I try not to get my feelings hurt."

My point is that every relationship is different and every person is different. And whether you want sex nine times a day or nine times a year, that isn't necessarily wrong. What is important is that you are communicating with your spouse in a way that is honest, open, and willing. If you're hurt about a perceived rejection, tell him. And if you feel like he wants sex about eight times a day too often, tell him that too.

Go All-Out for Sex Sometimes

I'm not an extravagant person.

I'm perfectly happy with plain-old normal coffee without pumpkin spice syrup or whipped cream. I'm perfectly happy wearing inexpensive clothes, using drugstore makeup, and eating burgers and fries. I've never even tried caviar. I like my simple life with my simple family and my simple tastes.

But for sex, I've come to the conclusion that it's okay to go all-out.

I may not need expensive clothes, but expensive bras and panties? Totally worth it.

And I may not need to eat in fancy restaurants, but for date night? Worth it.

And I'm perfectly happy sleeping in the Motel 6 for our family vacation, but if I'm going away overnight with my hubby? We upgrade. And it's totally worth the cost.

Of course I'm not telling you to break your budget for sex, but I am telling you that investing in an extravagant sex life from time to time is worth the cost. Because it's for your marriage. And your marriage is worth it. So book a night in that super romantic hotel downtown. Pay a babysitter for date night. Buy those black lace panties. Pick up that aromatherapy candle. And let your husband know that he's worth it.

A *Hot Mama* PLEDGE

I enjoy sex, so I will

- allow sex to be as important to me as it is to my husband.
- seek out my husband and show him that I also want sexual intimacy.

- refuse to talk about sexual intimacy in a way that's degrading or that makes it seem like it's just for my husband.

- honor God with my desires.

REAL *Hot Mama* IDEAS

"My husband was out hunting for four days. I was home with three kiddos and missing him very badly. As I knew he was preparing to come home, I sent him a text. It was a picture of his favorite racy thong underwear. I included a text that said, 'These seem like a good choice for today. What do you think? I can't wait to see you!' His reply: 'Mmmmm, that's my girl!' About an hour later he said via text, 'Sad. Leaving my happy place.' To which I replied, 'You are in luck, because another happy place awaits you.' He said, 'I love it when you do this to me.' It is funny that I don't do things like this more often—it takes very little effort on my part, yet it means a lot to him. It lets him know I desire him and try to prioritize our sex life. Sometimes by the end of the day, we are still too tired (let's face it: we have three kids that keep us running from sunup to way after sundown). But I think he likes to know that I care about sex. And something as simple as a fun, flirty game lets him know that I desire him."—T

"I jumped him when he got home. The kids were watching a movie and I just went for it."—N

"I often pray Proverbs 5:19 for my husband. I pray that he would become intoxicated with me, that he would desire every part of me: my breasts, my mouth, my heart, my soul—every part of me."—C

"This is totally crazy, but I booked a hotel for us for a midday splurge. I never do things like that, but we needed it. We just moved to a new town and I don't know any babysitters (so no date nights!). Plus, with the move and my husband's new job, our house was a mess and our evenings were spent unpacking boxes instead of making out. Finally, I'd had enough, so I showed up to his work and slipped down my shirt to show him I was wearing my red lacy bra. He told his boss he was taking the rest of the afternoon off to deal with some 'family things' and we drove straight to the hotel and spent the entire afternoon naked together. We left just in time to pick the kids up from school and it was worth every minute."—I

Hot Mama
"Good Girl Syndrome" BUCKET LIST

1. Tell your husband that you like having sex with him. Like right now. Walk over to him, kiss him, and tell him.

2. Read our ebook *10 Ideas to Inspire Red Hot Sex: A Hot Mama Challenge* and choose five challenges to do with your husband. Initiate every one.

3. Book a hotel for a night (or even an afternoon) away. Surprise your husband.

4. Try one of those "panty-of-the-month" clubs where they ship you cute undies in your size every month.

5. Plan a date night. And let him know you plan to have sex afterward.

6. Wake your husband up with a kiss . . . and a romp.

7

Get in the Mood

Do not deprive each other except perhaps by mutual consent and for a time, so that you may devote yourselves to prayer. Then come together again so that Satan will not tempt you because of your lack of self-control.

1 Corinthians 7:5

(Kathi)

I told Roger before we got married that it was in his best interest to never let me get too hot, too tired, or too hungry.

And if all three happened at the same time? Well, I couldn't be held responsible for my actions. Even with those conditions placed on my everyday life, it seems like Roger only wants sex when I am hot and tired. (The third condition can be solved pretty easily with the protein bar that's always in my bag.)

The thing is, usually when I'm *having* sex, I really enjoy it. But the *getting to having* sex? I'd rather rub cut glass than have him touch me. Especially if it's hot. Or I'm tired. Last summer was especially challenging in that way. It had been a winter of surgeries for both of us, and as soon as we were fully recovered, it felt like Roger wanted to make up for lost time.

I, on the other hand, was completely ready to take the summer off.

Normally I love it when Roger works from home. We can take a mid-afternoon walk with the dog, eat lunch together, and occasionally make a Starbucks run. But last summer I was so concerned that our afternoon lunch would turn into a nooner that I started suggesting that Roger work from the office.

In the last chapter, we talked about how it's okay for women to like sex. And to pursue sex. But that begs the question: What do you do when sex is the last thing on your mind and the first thing on his?

You get yourself in the mood, that's what.

I'm not saying you always have to be in the mood, but the Bible does explicitly say that as married couples, we shouldn't withhold sex from each other. (Check it out, the verse is 1 Cor. 7:5.) Which means that even if you're feeling too tired, too hot, too hungry, or too spit-up on, you probably still need to find a way to get yourself in the mood.

I think many, many women fall into the trap of what I call "the headache mentality." They are tired. They are feeling a bit—shall we say—overtouched. And a long massage followed by a good night's sleep sounds a whole lot better than hanky-panky.

So we fake a headache.

And after a while, headaches become more common than sex.

As we established in the last chapter: sex is awesome. God designed it just for us to enjoy with our husbands. It's a wonderful and beautiful thing. And it's certainly not something to fake a headache for. Save that for the next time your husband wants you to watch a Star Trek marathon.

Of course, knowing you should be in the mood and actually being in the mood are different things. So I'm dedicating this chapter to helping you (okay, helping us) get there. Because I know that in the end, it will be worth it. Just wait.

To be clear: I'm not saying you have to suddenly change who you are. And I'm definitely not saying you can't say no from time to time because you're tired and you've had three kids hanging on you all day and the last thing you want is to be touched more. In fact, I don't want you to change at all.

But I do want you to think.

Think about the last time you had sex with your husband. It was fun, right? And now think about how you felt afterward. I'm guessing you felt closer to him, like you had bonded in a way that no one else can bond with you. Maybe you fell asleep all snuggly warm. Or maybe you spent the night talking about how wonderful you are together.

Whatever you did and wherever you were, it was good, right? For both of you. Which is why I want to help you get into the mood (and stay in the mood) night after night after night.

Focus on Your Man

It's 10:00 p.m.

You have been going all day. Laundry. A work deadline. Diapers. Mac and cheese. School projects. Board meetings. A tough phone call from a friend. Whatever it is that you do all day, you've been doing it. And you're tired. And the last thing you want is to be going some more.

It's easy to focus on that ache in your shoulders, the (real) headache pounding behind your eyes, the fact that you feel like a frumpy old woman instead of a young hot mama.

But I don't want you to focus on that.

I want you to focus on your man. Turn and look at him right now. The guy who helped you scrub dishes after dinner. The guy who swept you backward for a kiss when he walked in the door and then lifted your daughter up for a piggyback ride. The same one who is smiling all crooked at you right now thinking you're beautiful.

He's who you're doing this for.

That kind of puts it in perspective, doesn't it?

Now go over there and do something about all of those feelings that you're having right now. It'll be fun.

Know the Power of Yes

I try to say yes as much as I can (because I really like it when Roger says yes to me in pretty much any area of our lives). I know that there are times when no needs to be okay, but most of the time, I make an effort to say yes. Even if I'm not quite feeling up for it.

Here are a few ways I can say yes, even when I'm not in the mood:

- **Delay it.** If Roger is finding me especially sexy, but I'm not feeling it, one thing I've done several times is to go take a shower and wash the day's grime off of me. That makes me feel 25 percent sexier instantly. I'll put on some lotion and then come out of the bathroom in a robe or some lingerie that I've stashed in the cupboard. As women we often need a little time to get into the same space that our husbands pretty much live in.
- **Ask for help.** I'll tell Roger, "Can we just snuggle for a while?" and that's my code for "I'm willing to go there with you, I just need some time and attention first." That's when the massages happen, or we neck extravagantly.
- **Fake it.** Fake it until you make it. Put on lingerie. Make out. Say yes even when you want to say no.

Plan for Sex

Several of my hot mama friends have told me that they have a regular night for sex. That whole day they know that sex is happening and they are preparing themselves (emotionally and shaving-wise) for the evening's activities. I love this idea.

Of course, some of my type B friends think that rigid scheduling is a bit of a mood killer, and if this is you, you can still plan for sex without actually scheduling it:

- Shower at eight o'clock in the evening. Once things are winding down at your house kid-wise and dinner-wise, hop in the shower, use some yummy-smelling shower gel, shave if you need to, and then put on some cute pajamas.

- Get rid of your unsexy panties. That means you'll have to wear sexy ones. Every day.
- Buy an aromatherapy candle. Light it.
- Pick up some massage gel. Use it.
- Think about sex during the day. As often as possible.
- Send your husband a sexy text message or two.

Always Say "Later"

This is pretty self-explanatory, but next time your husband wants sex and you're not in the mood, try saying, "Not tonight, but how about tomorrow?"

Then roll over and type a sex date right into your iPhone. Set a reminder. Make sure he knows that you mean it and you want to have sex with him and soon.

That way he won't feel like you're rejecting him, just postponing him.

And you'll have something fun to look forward to tomorrow.

A *Hot Mama* PLEDGE

I want to be in the mood for my husband, so I will

- choose to look at sex as something I want to have instead of something I want to avoid.

- make an intentional effort to be in the mood for sex for my husband.

- say yes as often as I can in order to help myself get in the mood more often.

REAL *Hot Mama* IDEAS

"I found myself faking a headache (or a stomachache or a too-tired ache) more often than not. I knew I needed to break the habit so I told my husband that I would have sex with him at least once a day for the next seven days no matter what. He did not object. And by the third day, I found myself looking forward to it."—S

"I started showering at night before I go to bed. Of course, oftentimes I have to shower again in the morning, but a few extra showers never hurt anyone. And showering certainly got me in the mood."—C

"My husband asked me to have sex last night and my gut response was 'not tonight' . . . but I bit my tongue and said 'maybe' and then asked if we could trade massages. Five minutes later, my mood had changed. Good thing I didn't say no."—U

"The first text I sent my husband was when I was in the driveway about to leave for work around 7:30 a.m.: 'Have I mentioned lately how handsome you are?' I kept it going throughout the day, sending a total of eleven texts. He started to respond around lunch. My final text was sent just prior to our son going to bed—just four words: 'Are you feeling frisky?'—while we were sitting side by side on the couch. I actually felt nervous about sending these texts—it's very unlike me. But it certainly got me in the mood. It also affected the mood of the night in general. There wasn't any stress preparing dinner, and the entire night was spent in playful banter as we took care of the usual evening tasks. And by the time our son went to bed, well . . ."—T

Hot Mama
"Get in the Mood" BUCKET LIST

1. Shave and wear hot mama underwear every day.

2. Buy the tools you need to be in the mood—whether it's music or massage oil or a candle, get it. And use it.

3. Text your husband right now and let him know that you are in the mood . . . even if you're not.

4. Send your husband a text message and let him know you want to have sex with him tonight.

5. Put sex on the calendar after you say no. Tell your husband, "I'm not feeling well tonight, but I'm writing your name in Sharpie for tomorrow night."

6. Next time you have a headache, have sex anyway. And consider how much you enjoy it.

7. Promise your husband you'll have sex every day for the next seven days. He'll hold you to it, we're sure.

Let's Talk about Sex, Baby

Let your conversation be always full of grace, seasoned with salt, so that you may know how to answer everyone.

Colossians 4:6

(Erin)

I'm a talker.

And so right after we got married, I figured that Cameron and I should probably have a nice, long conversation about sex. I put on my flannel pj's (the perfect sex-talk outfit in my mind) and plopped down on the couch right as *Monday Night Football* was starting. Okay, so my timing may not have been impeccable, but nonetheless, I was still shocked when he looked at me, blinked several times, stood up, walked to our CD case, and pulled out a CD.

My first thought was, *Oh, he wants some mood music.* I was mistaken. Because the words that blasted out of the boom box were from Toby Keith's song "A Little Less Talk and a Lot More Action."

Point taken.

After that, I was a little tentative when it came to talking about sex. I knew we should be talking about doing it in addition to doing it, but I also knew that Cameron wasn't the biggest fan of sex talks—even when I didn't schedule them smack in the middle of the third quarter.

I'll admit it: I withdrew. I chose to delay conversation or even avoid it in order to make sure I wasn't being the crazy wife who forced my husband into annoying conversation just because I wanted to talk about sex.

Then, a few months ago, I started writing our ebook *10 Ideas to Inspire Red Hot Sex*. I told him right away that I was writing a book and it was about sex, but I may have glossed over the details a teeny tiny bit.

You see, the ebook includes ten sex challenges. Totally fun, totally flirty things couples can do to make their sex lives sizzling hot. As I wrote the book, I recruited several of my friends to try out the challenges and give me feedback, but as I put the finishing touches on the book, I realized that I had roped all my friends into trying challenges, but I hadn't tried any myself.

I had to remedy that.

I walked into the room one night and gave Cameron my most sexy smile.

"Hey! Do you want to do a sex challenge?" I assumed—incorrectly—that he would get that goofy grin on his face right then and that would be the end of our little talk.

It wasn't.

"A sex challenge. What does that mean?" Leave it to Cameron to ask the mood-killing questions.

"So, uh, I'm working on this book where I'm, uh, challenging people to, uh, try out some fun, flirty things when it comes to sex."

"You're doing what?" He was absolutely shocked. (Apparently I had glossed over the main point of the ebook when I had explained it to him before.)

Let's just say we had a long, long conversation that night.

And for the record, there was no action later in the bedroom.

In retrospect, my being honest up front with him about (a) the book and (b) my feelings would have probably changed his reaction just a little bit. Sadly, I had backed myself into the awkward conversation corner, because I chose not to tell him what I was thinking, feeling, and writing about from the very beginning.

All that said, I'm writing this chapter for myself more than for you: I have to start talking to my husband about sex.

From now on, my song will be "A Little *More* Talk and a Lot More Action," because I need both talk and action. It's absolutely essential for my marriage that when I'm thinking about sex—no matter whether it's a positive or a needs-improvement issue—I need to talk to Cameron about it.

And you should probably do the same with your husband. Honestly. Openly. And as often as possible.

The Connection between Sex and Talk

There is a very fine line between sex and talk.

For Cameron and me, if everything is going well in our marriage, talking about sex often leads to sex (a good thing) and having sex often leads to talking about sex (also a good thing). But there are other times when things aren't running quite so smoothly.

Sex is a very vulnerable thing.

And because of that, if the lines of communication aren't open for one reason or another, your sex life isn't going to be as intimate. Likewise, if your sex life isn't as intimate as it should be for some reason, the lines of communication will close. Which is why we hot mamas have the important job of making sure our conversations about sex are uplifting, honest, and helpful. And a few tips can help us meet that goal.

Talk in the Living Room, Not in the Bedroom

It's a really, really bad idea to talk about sex in the bedroom. But you already knew that, didn't you?

The bedroom is where you are most vulnerable. You're laying it all out there, you're connecting at the deepest level, your entire being is laid bare.

This is not the place to talk about sex.

This is the place to have sex.

I strongly recommend (yes, I know from experience) that you save whatever conversations you need to have about sex for the living room—at a time when you're both wearing clothes. And save the bedroom for, well, bedroom stuff.

Give Very Gentle Suggestions

Okay, let's be honest: sometimes sex isn't quite as good as it should be. Maybe one of you isn't feeling quite as energetic as he or she should, or perhaps someone is trying out a new technique that is falling a bit flat. Whatever it is, there are times when sex is more vanilla than hot. It just doesn't work.

But having a conversation about sex when sex isn't quite working? It's completely awkward. And uncomfortable. I think I'd rather sort socks than talk about it. It's so important to have open and honest conversations about what's working and what's not when it comes to sex, but it's equally important to talk gently (very gently) about what will make things better.

Very gently is the operative phrase here. Try saying things like,

- "What if we were to try . . . ?"
- "I'd love it if . . ."
- "You are so good at *X*, maybe we could do that a little more."
- "I'm feeling . . ."
- "I love having sex with you so much that . . ."

With a little gentle finesse, you two can work together to make sex amazing for both of you.

Seek the Real Truth about Sex

Issues with guilt, past hurts, accountability, and sexual sin can be . . . well, they are certainly mood killers.

My friend N told me she realized that for years she had avoided talking to her husband about sex because she was afraid she wouldn't be able to handle the answers to her questions. She admitted to me that she worried that her husband was struggling with lust but was afraid that if she talked to him about it she would find out things that would make her feel incompetent as a wife.

She finally brought it up and his answer was far from the reality she had created in her head. He said that he did occasionally struggle with lust when he was dating, but he had gotten into an accountability group with some friends at church and they were helping each other to stay on track. Oh, and he reassured her that she was the only woman for him and that she need not worry.

I think a lot of times we let our imaginations carry us away, and then we create a truth in our minds that's far from true. Let your husband share the real truth. And then work through it together. Only by talking openly, honestly, and bravely can you get to a place of transparency and let go of the anxiety that comes with not knowing what your husband is thinking.

Celebrate Talking

Remember that story I told you earlier about when I put on my flannel pajamas and tried to talk to Cam about sex during *Monday Night Football*? In retrospect, I may have gotten that one a little bit wrong. In fact, I probably doomed that conversation for failure before it even started.

Yes, talking about sex can be awkward and uncomfortable. But it can also be intimate, enjoyable, and marriage building. And I choose the latter.

Next time you think you need to have a conversation about sex, why not make it enjoyable? Make a special dessert or open a bottle of wine. Light candles or the fire. Snuggle on the couch. Enjoy being together and talking about intimate things. And make it so next time you say, "Let's talk about sex, baby," your husband will say yes.

Have All the Conversations

"I wish there was a checklist of things that I should talk about with my husband," my friend M told me. "I'm willing to talk to him about sex," she went on, "but I don't even know where to start." (Plus, she admitted later that every time they start talking, they end up in bed before they can finish the conversation. Go, M!)

You (okay, M) asked, so we've delivered. Below is a list of sex conversation starters for you and your husband. Grab the list, head into the living room, and ask each other each question one by one. It may take a few nights to finish the list, but that's okay. Oh, and if you want to make your conversation a bit more flirty and fun, M's suggestion is to make a rule that you can have sex only after you've talked about one of these topics for fifteen minutes. And you have to set a timer and promise not to cheat.

10 Conversations about Sex That Every Couple Should Have

1. **Likes and dislikes.** What do you like about sex? What don't you like? What can I do to make sex more enjoyable for you?
2. **Confidence.** In what areas do you not feel confident in your body or performance? How can I help you to feel more confident?
3. **History.** What were your past sexual experiences? Is there anything that makes you feel guilty or ashamed when it comes to sex? How can I help you get over that?
4. **Limits.** Is there anything that makes you uncomfortable sex-wise? Is there anything you would rather not do?

5. **Romance.** What makes you feel sexy? What can I do to make you want to have sex with me? What shouldn't I do?

6. **Rejection.** If I can't have sex with you, how do you want me to tell you? What can I do to help you not feel rejected?

7. **Fantasy.** If I could give you your ultimate sexual experience, what would it be? What can I do to deliver that for you?

8. **Frequency.** How often do you want to have sex? Are we doing it too often, or not enough?

9. **Foreplay.** What gets you ready? How can I help you have the best sexual experiences?

10. **Planning.** How can we plan to fit more sex into our busy schedules? What can I do to make myself more accessible to you? How can we be creative so we can have more sex?

A *Hot Mama* PLEDGE

I want to have meaningful marriage-building conversations, so I will

- have open and honest conversations about sex with my husband.

- gently tell my husband what I'm thinking and feeling when it comes to sex.

- be willing to discuss issues in our sex life before they become problems.

REAL *Hot Mama* IDEAS

"My husband and I took a three-hour road trip to visit my in-laws, and on the way, the baby fell asleep in the backseat. Bingo! Time to talk about sex. I brought it up and we had a great conversation about our personal likes and dislikes. It definitely made things hotter in the bedroom for us."—L

"We have been really disconnecting when it comes to sex. It's actually good when we have it, but most nights we both are too tired and too stressed to even start. I knew we needed to have a talk, so I set the stage. My husband loves ice cream sundaes, so I picked up a bottle of chocolate syrup and after we put the kids to bed, we had a decadent dessert and a great conversation."—N

"We used your conversation list. We just ran down the list you wrote and asked each other each question. It started to feel a bit awkward to me (right around the 'limits' question) so I turned my back to him and snuggled against him. He rubbed my shoulders and something about not looking him in the eyes made me feel more open. Of course, when we were done I looked him straight in the eyes and told him how much it all meant to me."—H

Hot Mama
"Let's Talk about Sex" BUCKET LIST

1. Go through the list of sex conversation starters and talk about each one. (We highly recommend following M's suggestion and having sex afterward.)

2. Tell your husband what you want in bed (preferably when you're not in bed).

3. Make it a point to talk to your husband about sex around once a week—even if it's just to tell him how much you like having it with him.

4. Make a code word for sex so you and your husband can wink, wink, nudge, nudge talk about it without actually saying the words. (Yes, sometimes just a linguistic change makes all the difference.)

5. Set the scene for a great conversation about sex. Light candles, grab something you both like to drink, make chocolate-covered strawberries. Bring sexiness into your sex talk.

9

Speak Respect

Anxiety weighs down the heart,
but a kind word cheers it up.
Proverbs 12:25

(Kathi)

There we were, Roger and I, at this fancy dinner fund-raiser event.

And by fancy, I mean that neither of us was wearing jeans. We're from the Silicon Valley—where we wear everyday jeans every day and wear dress-up jeans for special occasions—so this was a big deal. Roger was wearing a sports coat (and looked pretty hot if you ask me) and I had pulled out all the stops: both hair and makeup were done—on the same day.

Roger and I spend a lot of time going to these kinds of events. It doesn't matter what the purpose is—fund-raiser, awards banquet, anniversary/birthday parties, wedding, you name it—we've not only attended, but we've happily indulged in the dry chicken and strained chatter as well.

And for the most part, overcooked meat aside, we really enjoy them. I love seeing my husband all dressed up. I love supporting a great cause. I love not cooking dinner for a night. But there is only one problem: you never know who you're going to sit with.

You want to sit with the "fun" couples. You know, the ones who genuinely like each other and have fun together and tell great stories and love to laugh with each other (and occasionally at a speaker who has been talking a little too long).

But is that ever who you end up sitting with? Of course not! It's always the "other" couple.

The other couple: you can tell they just had a fight about his tie before they got to the table. He doesn't want to be at the event, and she is forcing him in no uncertain terms.

And then they start talking and that's when the real fun begins.

"I told you we were going to be late, but you wouldn't listen to me."

"Sit up straight." (Really? Is he four?)

Then, directed at us and the other people sitting at the table: "Sorry we're late. I knew I should have packed for my husband."

And so what could've been a fun night is stained by an "unfun" couple.

Ugh. Is there anything—and I mean anything—that is more awkward than hearing a woman berate her husband in front of other people? (Okay, maybe a man doing it to his wife, but that's another book.)

What it tells the husband, and everyone who is within earshot, is, "You are of no value to me."

That's the last thing I want my husband to be feeling from me.

However, there is almost nothing more attractive on earth (to a husband and the people around him) than a woman who is speaking well of her man. Don't you love it when you hear someone speaking words of encouragement about and to someone they love?

I swear, it can make your man about three inches taller in the process.

And a mutually respectful relationship can bring passion and intimacy and trust to your sex life like nothing else.

Before I move on, I want to make one thing very, very clear: I know that using respectful words is much more easily said than done. I know that even with the best intentions, you will slip regularly. Erin told me that at New Year's resolution time a couple of years ago, she made a vow to speak only positive words to her husband for a week straight. She got up early on January 1 and prayed that she'd be able to speak encouragement to his heart. She prayed for tenacity and kindness and grace . . . and twenty minutes and one glass of spilled milk later, she caught herself saying, "Why don't you ever help me when . . ."

Using respectful, encouraging words is so simple in concept, but so hard in implementation. But it's also one of those things that gets easier with time. As the habit develops, you'll catch yourself slipping with compliments instead of slipping with negative words. Let's discuss a few of the ways you can get all hot mama with your words and bless your husband in the process.

Be Your Husband's Biggest Encourager

Guys love cheerleaders—especially when the cheerleader is their wife. With this in mind, one of the best ways to be a hot mama is to intentionally, specifically, and regularly be your husband's biggest encourager. But before you start telling him what a great provider and dad and husband he is, wait a second. Wouldn't it mean more if you were specific with your encouragement? You know, so he'll know you're talking specifically to him?

Yes, every man wants to know that he's a good provider, that he's a great dad, and that he is loved as a husband. But it's so much more meaningful when the praise is specific. Which of the following would he rather hear?

- "You're such a good provider!" *or* "Thank you for going to work every day, even when you don't feel like it. I know how important it is to you to take care of our family. I tell the kids every single day what an amazing man you are."
- "You are a great dad!" *or* "I love seeing you interacting with our son. He is going to grow up to be a great man because of you."
- "I love you." *or* "I love how you make me feel. I am better because I get to be married to you."

Praise Him by Using Sexy Words about Sex

Not to point out the obvious, but the word *sexy* pertains to sex. And so if you're going to pledge to talk respect and encouragement to your husband about his work life or his character, don't clam up when it comes to talking about sex. One of the best ways you can encourage your man (and your sex life!) is to tell him how much you enjoy having sex with him—both inside of and outside of the bedroom.

Build Him Up in Front of His Kids

We as wives have the power to speak words of truth into our husbands, and, in turn, call out the best in them. This is especially true when we encourage our husbands in front of others—especially their children.

"Aren't we blessed to have such a strong daddy?"

"The people at your dad's work love him because he is great at solving problems."

"Honey, thanks for being such a great husband. The kids and I always feel safe around you."

Encourage Him in Front of People He Respects

I've found that there are two kinds of women: women who tease their husbands in front of people their husbands respect, and women who build them up in front of those people.

My pastor told me a story about a couple who came up to the front to talk to him on a Sunday morning after the church service. It was his first time meeting the couple, and he always loved to greet people who were checking out our church. Things were going well until right in the middle of the conversation, when the wife leaned over to her husband and hissed, "Stop slouching!"

Is there any amount of slouching that would make a husband look as bad as what that wife just did to her man?

Whether it's your pastor, your parents, his boss, or your child's teacher, make sure to take extra care in choosing your words around people whom your husband respects.

Be Intentional and Purposeful in Your Encouragement

Roger's birthday was coming up, but the last thing he wanted to do was celebrate. The large tech firm he works for was having layoffs—again. And he was feeling extra vulnerable. He'd just finished up one major project at work and was transitioning into a new group where he wasn't well known. When it came to the "higher ups" making lists of who would stay and who would go, Roger didn't feel confident that he would make it onto a list that fell in his favor.

I knew that Roger was dreading his birthday (who wants to have a party to celebrate another year passing when you don't feel confident in where your life is going?), so I thought I needed to do something different that year to celebrate.

In advance I talked to all of our kids and let them know the plan: we would go around in a circle and let Roger know one reason he rocked. It didn't have to be long, but the ground rule was that there was no sarcasm allowed.

This felt kinda weird and risky.

After all, my kids are on the cusp of adulthood. This was new and uncharted territory. And while I would love to be able to say that we are the kind of family that sits around the fire reading our favorite Bible verses aloud and speaking words of affirmation into each other's lives, we aren't. We're more of a play-games-around-the-kitchen-table-while-threatening-to-punch-each-other-for-winning type of family.

When the night finally arrived, the birthday dinner was barbecued and served, "Happy Birthday" was sung, and the white cake with white buttercream frosting was presented.

I was getting more and more nervous about the whole "You Rock" idea and wished that I hadn't told any of the kids about it—but it was too late to abandon ship. I dove in:

"Roger, we wanted to do a little something different this birthday. You know you are so important to each of us, but sometimes we don't say why. Today, we want to tell you why 'You Rock.'"

I started off by telling Roger that he "rocked" because of the kind of man he is—faithful, smart, and the best dad and stepdad I know. (And of course, I was bawling the whole time—but in a good way.)

Next it was Roger's son Jeremy's turn: "Dad, I wouldn't be in college if it weren't for you. I don't know how many times you've stayed up late, helping me with my homework."

Now I'm on the floor in a puddle of tears.

Then it was my daughter Kimberly's turn: "Roger, when I was first interested in stage direction and theater, you gave me my first job working on the church production. I loved working with you and learned so much. If it weren't for you, I would be on a totally different path in school, and wouldn't know what I truly love to do."

At that point, I was a total mess. And Roger was crying. And so were the rest of the kids.

Then Shawn, Amanda's boyfriend, spoke. (I'd told him he could have a pass if he wanted, and I didn't expect him to actually speak because of his quiet personality.) "Roger, Amanda and I have learned so much from you and Kathi. You have the kind of home we want to have when we get married."

Yep. I was done in.

And so was Roger.

I couldn't breathe through all my tears. All the kids contributed and Roger was blown away. It was just the reminder he needed that he had six people behind him who loved him and knew the best things about him.

Now all of our family wants the "You Rock" part added to their own birthday celebrations. In fact, I've had rocks inscribed with "You Rock" on them for each person so they have their very own rock on their birthday.

But none of us will forget the reason this all started: because Roger Rocks.

A *Hot Mama* PLEDGE

I want to speak words of respect to my husband, so I will

- speak kind words to and about my husband when others are listening.

- use respectful language when talking to my husband when others aren't listening.

- never belittle my husband (even if he has forgotten to take out the trash twenty times).

- remember that the best way to change my marriage is to encourage my husband, not to discourage him.

REAL *Hot Mama* IDEAS

"I have a sign next to our bathroom that I made in MS Word. It simply says, 'I love you because . . .' and there is a long line under it. I framed it and put a dry erase marker on a string next to it. Every so often I write a new reason on the line. It wipes right off the glass so I can change it any time. He walks past it several times a day and has come to look forward to a new message."—S

"I call him my hero and mean it! I let him know that I appreciate very much the little things he does, like printing an article for me."—K

"I leave encouraging notes on his steering wheel."—N

"I write on his Facebook wall and let not only him but also his friends and family see how great I think he is!"—D

"I refer to him as 'My Man' when speaking or in Facebook posts. I see him stand a bit taller when I do. That makes me stand a bit taller too."—L

Hot Mama
"Speak Respect" BUCKET LIST

1. Send him a flirty (or downright sexy) text message at work. (Just make sure he's the only one who looks at his phone before you hit Send.)

2. Leave a Post-it note with a loving message in a new spot every day for a week. If you're really feeling ambitious, do it for a month.

3. Let him catch you talking nicely about him behind his back.

4. Pick up a blank journal and jot down one thing you love about him every time he crosses your mind. Keep the journal on his bedside table so he can read it often.

5. Come up with a secret word that means "I think you are hot." Use it often—both in front of others and privately.

6. Send a note of praise in his lunch telling him how much you adore him.

10

Keep Sex out
of the Locker Room

> Do not let any unwholesome talk come out of your
> mouths, but only what is helpful for building others
> up according to their needs, that it may benefit those
> who listen.
>
> Ephesians 4:29

(Erin)

I text with my friends N and T about sex.

I know it sounds very locker-room-ish, but it isn't. Not at all. Because we aren't texting about sex to talk about sex, but instead to help each other build our marriages. Here's an example of a recent text string:

T: My kids. It's like they have a plan to make me unhappy today.

N: They have meetings to plan revolts or something.

E: Maybe we call in reinforcements? A maid, a masseuse, and a personal chef would make things better. At my house at least.

T: That would definitely help.

N: I'm putting the kids in their pj's and making bedtime 6. Then . . .

T: You go girl.

E: Maybe it's early bedtime night at all of our houses? Hot mama vow time.

T: It's on.

And then there's this one:

E: Feeling mad at C right now. He came home late again . . . and now I'm all frustrated.

N: Right. We all have bad days. So what now?

E: Ummmm, I guess I go fix dinner.

T: Or maybe you order pizza. We all feel that pressure sometimes and need a break. I'd bet if you apologized and ordered pizza, all would be fine by the time the kids go to bed. Wink, wink.

M: Yep, pizza and sex. Make everything better.

These conversations make our marriages stronger. I know that no matter how I'm feeling—angry, tired, happy, excited, whatever—I can text N and T and they will respond in a way that drives me toward my husband. Notice in the text messages above—we were laughing and joking and even at times crying—but no matter what was said, every response had the same end point:

Your marriage is important.

Your husband is important.

You need to turn to him.

Talking about sex often feels taboo. My friend L wrote me a note and said, "In my house growing up, we never once talked about sex. My parents gave me a book about sex when I was in the eighth grade and told me to read it and that was how I learned about sex." Another friend of mine, T, told me that her staunchly religious parents refused to even hold hands in front of her. When she learned about sex from a friend, she asked them about it and they frowned at her as if she had done something wrong.

On the other hand, we are all bombarded with sex in the media every day. Like Kathi said in chapter 1, every magazine in the grocery store line and every commercial on TV seems to scream sex, sex, sex. Only these messages are anything but God-honoring.

There is a strange duality operating in our culture: sex tends to be labeled as a private thing that shouldn't be talked about at all, yet we have a sex-crazed media that constantly bombards us with sexual messages. And because of this, the idea of talking about sex feels very confusing. I've heard the questions over and over from women I've talked to as I've written this book:

"Is it okay to talk about sex?"

"Who is it okay to talk to?"

"Should my sex life be completely private?"

The answer to that question lies in the answer to another question: Does your conversation honor God's plan for sex?

If your conversations are driving you closer to God and to your spouse, if they are encouraging you to make your sex life and your marriage a priority and they are honoring God in the process, then it's fine. In fact, it's probably a good thing.

But if your conversations become disrespectful in any way, if they demonize sex or your husband, if they are causing a wedge in your marriage or causing you to think about sex in a way that's anything but God-honoring, then they need to stop.

So how can we find that balance in our conversations? How can we make talking about sex less taboo so that we as Christian women can have intentional, accountable conversations about sex that help us to maintain a higher standard for marriage? Answers to those questions and more, coming right up.

Choose Friends Who Make Your Marriage Stronger

I told you earlier that I give my friends N and T credit for helping make my sex life stronger. Yes, they are very proud.

With our little sex accountability group, I know that I will always find listening ears and honest words, but never be led to talk about sex in a disrespectful way.

Not all friendships are like that.

I went to lunch with a friend a while back. Regrettably, I was in a bad mood and I started telling her about a fight Cameron and I had. She told me point blank: "You need to just leave your husband. We'll have so much fun as single girls." Now, she was going through her own little man-drama at that point and was in a place where she assumed all men were pure evil, but as soon as she said it, I made a mental

99

note to myself to never, ever talk to her about my husband again.

Regardless of the mistakes my husband makes or the problems we have, I love him. And I want my marriage to work. So I have to choose friends who want the same.

Think about your friends for a minute: are there certain ones who drive a wedge between your husband and you? Those aren't the women you should be talking to about your husband.

The friends you talk to about your husband should say things like:

"Yes, I'd be mad too, but he's worth going back to."

"Yes, I know you are tired and exhausted, but he's worth staying awake for."

"Yes, he bought you a Crock-Pot for your birthday, so make him a pot roast. (And if you're feeling really frisky, wear nothing under your apron.)"

Those are the friends who will strive for your marriage with you. The friends who will hold you accountable to always lean in to your marriage—and to never stop fighting for it.

Never Say Negative Things about Sex

I'm just going to come out and say it: it's very easy for us to fall into a pattern of bashing sex. I've heard the conversations. I probably even participated in them before I knew better.

"He rolled over again with those puppy dog eyes. I had to fake a headache for the fourth day in a row."

"Maybe if he started doing the laundry, I'd start doing him."
You might laugh, but comments like these are anything but funny. Sex is too important to make fun of, and our husbands are too loved, adored, and respected to tease like this. So can we just make a promise now to stop talking about sex in a way that's degrading and start talking about it in a way that's loving?

Allow Yourself to Be Held Accountable

Ask a friend or two to hold you accountable for sex. I believe that if you are getting busy less than once a week, and it's not an issue that you are seeing a professional about, you need an intervention. (Unless your husband is also perfectly happy with twice a month, then carry on, friend . . .)

Your friends can provide that intervention.

After the nooner incident that I described in the introduction of this book, I asked my friend N to hold me accountable to have sex. She challenged me to have my own nooner as quickly as possible. I resisted. But a few weeks later, I was sitting at home working while the kids were in school and I decided to just do it.

I texted Cameron: "Nooner?"

His response: "What? I mean, yes! See you in five."

When I told N and T about our little midday sex escapade, they both responded with jubilation. Because they know the secret: hot mamas don't let their friends have boring sex lives.

Encourage Your Friends to Be Hot Mamas

My friend S told me about a MOPS meeting at her church where the speaker (a seventy-year-old woman) walked around the room and gave each woman a little sticker that said "Good job!" or "Well done!"

"Does everyone have a sticker?" she asked.

"Yes." The women looked at her confused. Was she some ex-kindergarten teacher who was a little off her rocker?

"Good! Now I want you to go home and put your sticker somewhere on your body. When you next see your husband, tell him there is a surprise for him hidden somewhere on your body. Then tell him to find it."

The women burst out laughing. But then most of them went home and did exactly what the speaker had told them to do. S said the conversation at their MOPS table the next week was very animated as the girls described their husbands' reactions and the wonderful time they had.

We can be that kind of encourager for our friends:

- Encourage each other to go on date nights.
- Offer to trade babysitting or playdates.
- Go shopping together for lingerie.
- Tell each other our best sex tips.
- Never let friends fall into the headache routine.
- Remind each other of how much we love our husbands and how much we love sex.
- Give each other stickers and push each other to have a bit of fun with our sex lives.

A *Hot Mama* PLEDGE

Sex is something that should be talked about in a God-honoring way, so I will

- be God-honoring in every conversation I have about sex, putting my relationship with my husband as my top priority no matter what is said.

- find friends who hold me accountable as I strive to build a strong marriage.

- never talk about sex in a way that's degrading, disrespectful, or dishonoring of God.

REAL *Hot Mama* IDEAS

"I brought up sex at my MOPS table. We've never talked about sex before as a group so the start of the conversation was a little awkward, but we ended up having a great discussion. We even promised to continue the conversation next time."—C

"I was having coffee with my friend and she made a joke about her husband wanting sex all the time. I remembered this pledge and turned to her and said, 'I wish my husband wanted sex more often! It's such a wonderful thing.' This led to a great conversation about women's attitudes toward sex. She even told me thank you and said she was going to go home and initiate things with her husband that night."—L

"My best friend and I talk about everything . . . just not sex. I emailed her a little bit ago and told her that I wanted to change that. I asked her to hold me accountable to not only have sex, but also to talk about sex and my husband in a way that's edifying. She responded with a very encouraging yes and asked me to do the same."—F

"My friends in my MOPS group and I made a promise to never bash our husbands about sex. We realized that it had become a little habit of ours and we stopped. Instead, we replace those conversations with conversations about how great our husbands are. It has made a big difference—not only at our table, but also in my marriage where I'm suddenly looking for opportunities to have sex instead of to avoid it."—S

Hot Mama
"Out of the Locker Room" BUCKET LIST

1. Ask one or two of your closest friends to pray for your marriage and your sex life.

2. Start a marriage series (try *Sheet Music* or *Marriage on the Rock*) with your small group at church. Be willing to go deep.

3. Email one or two of your closest friends and ask them to hold you accountable for having sex more often.

4. Share creative ideas and sex tips with your friends. Ask them to share back.

5. Read this book (or another book about sex) with a few friends and help each other to talk about the important takeaways.

6. Start a hot mama accountability group. Promise to hold each other's marriages up to a high standard when it comes to sex.

7. Make a pact with your friends not to complain about sex.

11

Heat Things Up

How beautiful your sandaled feet,
  O prince's daughter!
Your graceful legs are like jewels,
  the work of an artist's hands.
Your navel is a rounded goblet
  that never lacks blended wine.
Your waist is a mound of wheat
  encircled by lilies.

  Song of Songs 7:1–2

(Erin)

My friend Hildi gave me an apron for a wedding present.

This wasn't just any apron. Picture the apron June Cleaver wore as she cooked pot roast, with an extra layer or two of hand-stitched lace and some blue calico fabric, and you'll have a decent idea of what it looked like.

Now, you're probably thinking that Hildi was trying to infuse a little 1950s housewife into my modern-college-student mindset and tell me gently that I might want to learn to cook something other than cereal.

But no.

She gave it to me so I would heat things up in my marriage.

You know that Garth Brooks song "Somewhere Other Than the Night"? The one where the farmer comes in from the field and his wife is standing in the kitchen stirring her pot roast with nothing but her apron on? No? Well, it was a great song released way back in the day, and Hildi and I used to sing it at the top of our lungs in our dorm room and then giggle on our bunks about what it would be like for—gasp!—a man to find us in the kitchen wearing nothing but an apron and whisk us away to who knows where for some romance.

When I got engaged, I immediately started thinking about all of the fun and romantic and sexy things I could do now that I would be married and it would be . . . permissible.

I'm fifteen years on the other side of that. And thinking back, I get a little sad. Because while I did wear that apron in the way it was intended (several times, *thankyouverymuch*), I have to confess that I've probably used it more often to cook. In fact, as I type this, it's hanging in my kitchen pantry sporting a big gravy stain on the lapel.

Garth Brooks would be so ashamed.

My pretty blue apron mocks me every time I walk into the pantry, taunting me with proof that we've turned the heat way (way) down since we entered the married-with-kids phase of our lives. Which, while normal, isn't what I want for my relationship or my sex life. I'm guessing you don't either.

What if you were to step outside of the proverbial bedroom—okay, the literal bedroom—and get busy elsewhere? What if you were to slip on some sexy lingerie, light a fire, put on that apron, and whip up a soufflé—or a bowl of cereal? What if? Kathi and I both believe that sex can be . . . sexy. And fun. As hot mamas, we have not only permission but also motivation to turn up the heat in our marriages.

Making a Habit of Flirty Fun

Ladies, I know I'm preaching to the choir when I say that a passionate and intimate sex life is part of God's gift to married couples. But allow me to let you in on a little secret: it's okay to have a bit of fun with it too. If that means slipping on a cute pair of panties and flashing a little bit of leg as you walk down the stairs after tucking the kids in bed, well, then by all means, show some leg. You might even want to get a pair of fishnet stockings to amp it up a little.

Part of the joy of being married is that you and your husband can have a little bit of flirty fun together. In Kathi's book *Happy Habits for Every Couple*, she says, "Your husband is designed by God to enjoy seeing you scantily clad, and you're the only one who can allow him to enjoy this very special, fun, and flirty experience."[1] With that in mind, amping up the heat should be simple. Easy. Natural. But it's not, is it?

It's hard to feel sexy when you're, well, not feeling sexy. I can think of several times in my married life when I have felt less than adequate in the sex-appeal department. After I weaned my daughter, my breasts—how do I say this delicately?—well, they shriveled. I remember trying on one of my pretty bras and my poor tired breasts couldn't even halfway fill it up. I wanted to cry.

Other times, I've felt tired. I've felt lacking. I've felt fat. I've felt cranky. I've felt . . . well, you get the picture. Sometimes we don't feel hot. But that doesn't mean you aren't hot. And that doesn't mean you can't have a steamy-hot sex life. That's what this chapter is about—taking things to the next level and helping you heat things up. Here are our heat-it-up ideas.

Just Do It

I don't want to overstate the obvious, but the first step to hopping on that horse is to hop on that horse. And, you're never going to enjoy the ride if you don't get onto the saddle. (Ba dap, ching!) Okay, okay, I'll stop with the cheesy metaphors, but you get my drift. You have to turn up the thermostat if you want things to get hotter.

So, tonight (yes, right now, today, this exact evening) I'm challenging you to just do it. Do something hot and sexy and totally unlike the you who spends her days in yoga pants. Do something like the honeymoon you. I don't know what it is . . . Maybe you change into that adorable panty-and-bra set you got for your wedding and wear it under your clothes. Let your robe slip off of your shoulders as you walk into the room after the kids go to sleep. Take the *Frozen* soundtrack off of your playlist and put Norah Jones on. Do something a little bit different. A little bit hot. A little bit . . . warmer than missionary-between-the-sheets. And give your husband the gift of a fully confident and fully beautiful you.

Don't Be Afraid to Do Something That's a Little "Out There"

It's really easy for couples to slip into white-sheets boring when it comes to sex. Oftentimes, it's not even intentional, but an exhausting week at work here and a long after-dinner conversation there and all of a sudden, sex becomes a ho-hum routine of the same old, same old. But in order to heat things up in true hot mama style, you have to be willing to try something new, something different, something . . . hot.

It was during one such ho-hum sex slump that I was—let's call it *inspired*—to invite my husband out onto our covered patio on a stormy night. And by stormy night, I mean that Hurricane Hermine had rushed into Austin in full force with driving rain, glowing lightning, and booming skies. But the back corner of our patio was sheltered from the storm's wrath, so Cameron and I snuggled on our patio furniture and watched the sky flash for hours. And let's just say that had my third son been a girl, I would have considered the middle name Hermine.

The point is that it's okay—no, more than okay, great—to do something a little frisky with your sex life. As long as both of you are comfortable we see no problem with experimenting a little with where you have sex, when you have sex, and how you have sex.

Change Your Outlook on Lingerie

I used to have this strange idea that if I didn't look like a Victoria's Secret model in my underthings then I was wearing them wrong. But one thing I've learned lately on Facebook (thank you article about Photoshop airbrushing) is that even the Victoria's Secret models don't look like Victoria's Secret models in lingerie.

To feel confident in lingerie you have to change your outlook. Instead of thinking of lingerie as something to make you look sexy, think of it as the ultimate camouflage so that you can *feel* sexy. Let it hide those birthing hips and give those saggy breasts a lift so that you, in turn, can focus on, well, what you want to be focusing on.

Get Some New Pajamas Already

I'll be the first to admit that every night is not a red-negligee night. But every night is an opportunity for you to show your husband that you love him and that he matters to you. And with that in mind, I'm going to ask you to do something very, very difficult. I'm going to ask you to throw away your ratty grey sweats with the coffee stain on the thigh.

I know, I know, they are so comfy and you've had them since you were in college and you wear them every time it's raining and . . . you have to get rid of them. Because your husband deserves better. If you wouldn't wear them in front of your neighbors or to the supermarket, you shouldn't wear them in front of your husband.

Once the sweats have hit the trash can, I'm going to ask you to invest in a few nice pairs of pajamas that you can wear on quiet evenings at home with your husband without looking like you just got run over by a tornado of Goldfish-crumb-spewing toddlers. Preferably these pajamas will be silky and soft and a little bit form-fitting and may even have some easily accessible buttons down the front so that they can quickly transition if a pajama-on-the-couch night suddenly turns into a red-negligee night.

Whatever you buy, buy it with the intention of showing your husband that he matters to you and that the way you look for him is just as important as—no, wait, make that more important than—the way you look for others. And that you're willing to go the extra mile even if he's the only one who is going to see you.

A *Hot Mama* PLEDGE

I want a hot, sexy sex life, so I will

- be intentional about making my sex life an important part of our marriage.

- work to make sure that our sex life is fulfilling for both my husband and me.

- realize that a hot marriage is a gift from God and is something to be embraced.

- have fun in my sex life!

REAL *Hot Mama* IDEAS

"I have this teeny tiny red thong that my husband just loves. Whenever I want to really make him smile, I put it on under my jeans and then flash a tiny bit of the red fabric to him as I'm making dinner or getting the kids ready for bed. Let's just say he usually helps me with the dishes on those nights."—S

"I buy a really sexy nightie every year for my husband's birthday, wrap it, and leave it under his pillow. I think he might look forward to that gift more than he looks forward to cake!"—T

"Last year, a woman came to my MOPS group and talked about the importance of having fun in our marriages. So the girls at my table took action. We planned a panty exchange—each of us drew the name of someone else at the table and picked them out a sexy pair of panties. We had a big party and opened our new lingerie, and then encouraged each other to use it to bring some fun and excitement into our marriages."—I

Hot Mama
"Heat Things Up" BUCKET LIST

1. Go shopping with your husband and pick out some cute lingerie that you both like. (My friend N said that she did this with her husband once and he shocked her by choosing plain white lace. She said she changed her lingerie purchases from that date forward.)

2. Feed the kids an early dinner and put them to bed before your husband comes home. Let him come home to candlelight, a romantic dinner, and . . . you.

3. Wear cute panties under your everyday clothes. Yes, even a thong.

4. Have sex outside. (For the record, we highly recommend somewhere private and dark.)

5. Try the old trench coat trick—let him catch you wearing a trench coat with only something slinky underneath. Or you could try an apron.

6. Text your husband and ask him to join you for a nooner.

7. Toss out all of your old ratty underwear. Leave him a note asking if he'd like to help you pick out new.

8. Book a night in a hotel for you and your man.

9. Wear your honeymoon lingerie again . . . even if it's totally out of style or doesn't quite fit as well as it used to.

12

Knowing Your Man

There is no fear in love. But perfect love drives out fear, because fear has to do with punishment. The one who fears is not made perfect in love.

1 John 4:18

(Erin)

My text message signal buzzed just as I was pulling into the school parking lot to drop off my kids.

It was from Kathi.

"Love you, Baby! I'm so proud of who you are!"

I have to admit that my first thought was, *Why is she calling me Baby?* But immediately after that I got all fluttery about how sweet she was being to send me a text saying she was proud of me. And telling me how much she loved me. I wrote her back and said, "Awwww, thanks!"

She wrote back and said, "Whoops! It's true. But that was meant for Roger. I say the exact same thing to you. Just not with the Baby."

And I was totally deflated.

Just kidding! I was so entirely impressed that Kathi was sending such a sweet, honoring, kind, amazing text to her husband. I really shouldn't have been surprised. Kathi is the kind of wife who kisses her husband as he walks through the door—with a pot roast in one hand and a come-hither look in her eye. But her little texting mishap made me think: I need to reread the respect chapter Kathi wrote. And I need to be more affirming to my husband.

So I tried the same thing. I picked up my phone and texted Cameron: "Love you, Baby! I'm so proud of who you are!"

His response: "Who did you mean to send that to?"

So apparently I'm not quite as affirming as I should be.

On top of that, my pot roast, well, it leaves something to be desired. I just can't figure out how to make the meat tender without making the vegetables mushy. (Someone help me!)

And I don't think I've worn a come-hither look in my eye since 2008.

Suddenly, I sank into this mushy, muddled pit of self-pity as I considered what a good wife Kathi is (she's a total rock star) and what a terrible, awful, no good, very bad wife I am.

Poor me, right?

But here's the thing: Cameron isn't really a words of affirmation guy. This is evidenced by the fact that he (a) rarely reads his text messages, (b) rarely writes them, and (c) hasn't sent me a mushy love note since, well, ever. That's not to say I shouldn't speak respect to him—I should—but maybe that shouldn't be my focus. He is a quality time guy. And a physical touch guy. So to him, the perfect wife may not send him lovey-dovey text messages, but she certainly carves out time to go with him to the game—and gives him a little hug when she sees him.

As Cameron's wife, I want to do everything I can do to be the best wife for Cameron. So I have to take every expert tip, morsel of advice, or friend's solution with a grain of salt. Because none of those people is married to Cameron.

And none of those people knows him like I do.

As I work to become the hot mama wife of his dreams, my first focus has to be him. Not me. Not others. Not a list of shoulds and shouldn'ts. But him.

Just him.

And my really amazing lasagna.

I was telling Kathi about how my husband wasn't very impressed with my text message, and she, in all of her hot mama wisdom, said, "Well, that just means you have to figure out what encourages him." Kathi's right. We are all married to different guys and part of being married to your man is figuring out what makes your man tick. For some it may be a cute text message. For others it may be cute underwear.

God created you to be the best wife for your man. Regardless of your strengths and weaknesses, you have everything it takes to be the wife your man needs. So let's talk about some areas to focus on to help you know your husband even better, especially when it comes to sex.

Know What Turns *Your* Husband On

Kathi and I were talking to a couple of women about dressing to please our husbands. One of the women said her husband loves it when she's dressed to the nines, wearing heels and a little black dress. Another woman gave the standard lingerie answer. And I told them that Cameron loves me in a tight pair of jeans and a T-shirt.

Kathi's answer? Roger doesn't care what she's wearing on the bottom—even if it's ratty sweats—as long as she's wearing a Mickey Mouse shirt. It turns out that Roger's love of Disneyland carries over into every area of his life.

I can say with some level of certainty that Cameron wouldn't be quite as excited about seeing me in a Disney shirt. But a University of Texas shirt? That would be a different story.

Make it your mission to figure out what turns your husband on and then do that thing often. If it's Disney shirts, buy one for every day of the week. If it's sexy lingerie, then sign up for one of those lingerie-of-the-month shipments. And if it's Texas Longhorn shirts, well, since I'm certain everyone reading this is already a die-hard fan, you probably already own enough of those.

Never Compare

I used to have a WWKD habit. WWKD, obviously meaning, *What Would Kathi Do?* And can you blame me? Let me remind you: Kathi is a really good wife. She genuinely adores Roger and does sappy romantic things like send him cute text messages about how proud she is of him during the day.

But, as I explained earlier, WWKD didn't help me much. Because Cameron isn't Roger.

And the things that Kathi does don't exactly resonate with Cameron like they do with Roger.

We just can't be comparing ourselves to other women. Maybe one of your friends works outside the home and earns a billion dollars a year to contribute to her household. Or maybe one of your friends cooks a homemade and healthy dinner every night. I'm sure you know a woman or two who wears lingerie on a daily basis. One of your friends may wear a size 0, or a size 34 DD bra.

Whatever it is, that's great for your friends.

But it's not necessarily great for you.

Let me be clear: You will never measure up to everyone else's standards. But you can certainly be everything God created you to be for your husband.

Aim to please God and him—and forget about everyone else.

Figure Out How to Comfort *Your* Husband

Cameron was having a tough week at work.

I tried rubbing his shoulders. (He said he was too tense for a back rub. What's up with that?) I tried doing his laundry. I tried being there for him to talk to. (He watched football and tuned me out.)

I started to worry that I was failing as his wife. But then I realized: I just hadn't hit his sweet spot. Literally. I remembered him telling me about this amazing chocolate–peanut butter torte that his mom made when he was a kid. He told me that once, after he got a concussion on the football field, his mom had made him that torte and he had sat around all week eating it straight out of the springform pan as he watched the game tape. Apparently that had made him feel better.

I called his mom and got the recipe.

And that night after the kids were in bed, I pulled the entire pan out of the fridge along with a fork and handed it to him while he watched football. For the first time that week, he not only smiled, but he turned off the TV. And we finally connected.

It's easy to fall into the pattern of doing the things we've always done—helping in the ways that we *think* will help instead of in the ways that actually do. So, next time your husband is struggling, I want you to push aside all thoughts of the things you have always done and instead rack your brain for a sentimental way that you can touch just him.

Listen Aggressively

My mom told me that when my brother Troy was little, he was the strong, silent type (read: he had two sisters who talked nonstop, so he tended to retreat). She said she started to worry that she didn't know him, so she tried to figure out how to get him to talk. The answer? In the evenings after everyone else was asleep, she'd head into his room and find him in his bed reading comic books. She'd sit down and suddenly he would spill his guts.

I'm married to a strong, silent type. (It turns out that many men in my life tend to be quiet. I'm sure it has nothing to do with my personality.) Cameron could go days without talking if I let him. So I've made it my personal mission to figure out what makes him want to communicate, then do whatever it takes to get him to talk.

And I listen.

Why? Because if I don't know him, it's a lot harder to speak his love language.

In order for us to effectively reach our husbands, we have to know who they are. For us to know who they are, we have to give them space to talk to us. And to give them space to talk to us, we have to know what makes them want to talk.

Practice Being a Good Wife

Remember when I said that God made you the best wife for your husband?

You are.

But practice is what leads to excellence. That means the more you practice being the best wife for your husband, the more likely you are to become exactly the wife your husband needs. Here are a few things you can do to practice:

- Pray for your husband.
- Pray for yourself as a wife. Ask God to show you what your man needs from you.
- Seek out ways to make him smile.
- Figure out his love language. (If you need help, check out Gary Chapman's book *The Five Love Languages*.)
- Tell him how much you love him.
- Be slow to get angry.
- Be quick to apologize.
- Be willing to give him as much time and energy as he needs.
- Compliment him often.
- Have sex with him whenever you can.
- Learn about new things together.
- Invest time in getting to know him—his hopes, his dreams, his heart.
- Allow him to know you.

A *Hot Mama* PLEDGE

I want to be the best wife possible for my man, so I will

- figure out what speaks love to my husband and do that often.
- focus on my own gifts and make sure that I use them to honor my husband and God.
- stop comparing myself to other wives.
- do things every day to make sure my husband knows that I love him.

REAL *Hot Mama* IDEAS

"I'm not a chef, but my husband loves his mom's enchiladas. So I asked her for the recipe and made them for him. He was thrilled. I even made an extra pan for the freezer so we could have them again."—W

"My husband always seems to want to chat with me in the mornings. I am not a morning person, so this usually results in me covering my head with a pillow and groaning at him. But this morning, I set my alarm and got up and made coffee. When he woke up, I handed him a cup and we had the best conversation. I will have to do that more often."—D

"I started texting my husband words of encouragement. I expected him to feel loved, but what I didn't expect was that it would change the way he treats me. He is an avid hunter, and archery deer season is in full swing, so most weekend days he has been up and gone to the woods for a few hours before I roll out of bed around eight. But this morning, at 8:20 a.m. I received a text from HIM, which is unusual. It was playful and said, 'Good morning tooty fruity.' This is totally out of character for him, and when he got home, we spent the rest of the day flirting."—T

Hot Mama
"Knowing Your Man" BUCKET LIST

1. Call your husband's mom and ask her what his favorite food was when he was a kid. Make that dish for dinner.

2. Ask your husband what he likes you to wear. Wear those clothes on a date night—even if they aren't the most comfortable or flattering in your opinion.

3. Set aside time just to talk. Even if he's not opening up, listen aggressively.

4. Pray that your husband would learn to be open, honest, and brave with you.

5. Turn your husband on. Wear lingerie. Set the stage. Kiss him passionately. Let him know that you want him.

6. Encourage your husband every day. Tell him—or show him— why you love him and what makes him the right man for you.

13

What Happens in the Bedroom, Happens in Our Bedroom

> My people will live in peaceful dwelling places,
> in secure homes,
> in undisturbed places of rest.
>
> Isaiah 32:18

(Kathi)

I love our bedroom. We have a California King bed with a cream duvet and stacks of comfy pillows. The room is painted in a light almost-white lavender (yes, Roger approved the color) and has touches of deep purple on the curtains and throw pillows. We have (very expensive) blackout shades since the room is in the direct line of sight for the morning sun. The only other thing besides the shades that we've "invested" in for our home is our mattress. Our mattress is the best we could afford.

Sleep and sex are that important to us.

And not necessarily in that order.

Now, after describing what I did above, you're probably imagining my master bedroom as some sort of a retreat straight out of the movies. And it is. Halfway. Because all of the stuff I mentioned above is crammed into half of the room. The other half? My giant wraparound desk and a recording setup for our podcast.

Not super-conducive to the retreat-like feel that most home-decorating magazines are trying to promote, is it?

With varying groups of (big) kids living in our smallish home with Roger and me, our master bedroom always had to serve as a multipurpose room. Besides being the place where Roger and I sleep, it has also served as a

- home office
- laundry-folding area
- TV-viewing room
- kid-bonding room
- recording studio

As much as I would love to make our bedroom a full-time sanctuary for me and my husband, the idea of moving into a bigger house (and taking on a bigger mortgage) would have put more of a strain on our marriage and given us a little less "alone time." So, we improvise.

Yes, that's right. We don't give up on having a sexy retreat because we don't have the space. And we certainly don't throw out any chance of a sexy boudoir just because we have piles of laundry around. Instead, we make it work with what we have. And, with the right set of tricks (and some very intentional rules), our master bedroom really is the retreat that we need.

Even with the podcasting equipment in the corner.

With a little help, you too can build your own private, romantic, intimate, and sexy world with your husband so that the two of you can share life in a way that only a married couple can.

Fully, enjoyably, and as God intended.

Making a Place to Connect

I would love to design the perfect romantic bedroom for Roger and me. Satin sheets, luxurious bedding, those fancy lightbulbs that make you look twenty pounds thinner. (Wait. They don't exist? Someone really should invent some.) It would be amazing. But honestly? I think that it's a bit more important that we're (a) able to pay the mortgage and (b) able to do things like eat food and pay the bills each month. We simply can't afford to go off and spend $400 on a set of 1,235,325-thread-count sheets.

But just because we don't have the money (or, as I mentioned above, the space) to design a perfect master retreat, doesn't mean we can't make our bedroom pretty special. Because (laundry piled on the bed aside), we have everything we need to make our bedroom a place of connection. We just have to make sure to do it.

Have What You Need

I'm going to go ahead and assume that you have a bed in your bedroom. (If not, well, girl, you really need to go shopping.)

But aside from a bed, there are other necessities to a perfect master bedroom. Here are some other things you need:

- **A bedroom lock.** For obvious reasons, if you have kids.
- **Nice bedding.** Crunchy, scratchy, dirty, or otherwise unattractive bedding isn't conducive to sex.
- **Mood lighting.** Or lack of lighting altogether. I'm sorry, you just can't have sex under glaring fluorescent bulbs. So either tone them down or turn them off.
- **Space to move.** Nothing (well, maybe except for kids) will put a damper on your sex life more than a pile of clutter in the middle of your bed.

Delete What You Don't Need

There are plenty of things you do need in a sexy retreat, but there also are plenty of things you don't. Namely kids. And iPads. And, well, I'll just go ahead and write you a list:

- **Chores.** I'm not saying you can't do these things in your master bedroom, but you should always have a hideaway plan. In my master bedroom, laundry goes on top of the washer, bills get tucked in a drawer, and my work to-do list gets turned upside-down.
- **Technology.** I admit, I have technology in my bedroom (remember, the room doubles as an office). But, I make sure that I shut it down after six o'clock. If I want to keep working, I just take my laptop somewhere else in the house. It's a great habit that has kept me from staying up way too late reading Facebook posts and Instagram.

- **Kids.** My daughter Kimberly would sometimes want to hang out with me in our room for an episode of *Gilmore Girls* (okay, most likely to escape the boys of the house). And I loved curling up on the bed with her, popcorn bowl between us, connecting. But we had a rule that after 5:00 p.m., when Roger got home from work, the room was his and mine.

- **Pictures of the kids.** My friend I says that the first thing she does when she hops in bed is reach over to her nightstand and lay the smiling picture of her baby on its face. She says that seeing his face makes her feel maternal and nostalgic, but not sexy.

- **Television.** I admit it: we have a TV in our bedroom. Like I said, we used to turn it up loud when we wanted to have alone time and there were kids in the house. And we still use it to watch movies while snuggled in bed. But we also have strict boundaries around the TV: no sci-fi for Roger or *Project Runway* for me unless the other is watching as well.

Keep Things Nice

I get it. Sometimes money/time/space/energy/budget/kids/chores stand in the way of keeping your house nice.

I mean, if money, time, space, energy, budget, kids, and chores didn't stand in my way, my master bedroom would be perfect. We'd have a big old four-poster bed with gorgeous handmade silk linens from Italy. There would be a roaring fireplace in the corner and a marble hot tub in the bathroom and views of towering mountains just outside.

It would be perfect.

But for the record, money, time, space, energy, budget, kids, and chores all stand in my way. And my master bedroom is evidence. It's lovely, but not perfect. It's quaint, but not majestic. But it's right for us.

All that said, I want you to find the fine line between "perfect" and "shoddy." Erin told me when she first got married, they slept on an old, full-sized mattress that was thrown on the floor. They had no fitted sheet, so a regular white sheet was thrown on top of that and an old comforter on that. Not sexy. At all.

And while I get that finances are tight, that space is small, that kids and laundry tend to pile into your room, I want to encourage you to make your master bedroom nice. Make sure you've allowed the necessary budget to have a few essentials (sheets and a bed, to name a couple), and make sure you've kept your room clean enough that you don't step on Legos or garbage when you get out of bed.

It makes a huge difference when your bedroom is sex-worthy.

And, in case no one has told you, that is kind of the point.

You Are the "Sexy" in Your Sexy Bedroom

I have never felt good about lingerie.

But then I married Roger. Not surprisingly, Roger did not have the same disdain that I did for lingerie. In fact, quite the opposite.

So I did what any bride would do: I bought some lingerie for the wedding night, and then figured that as long as I eventually took off my flannel pj's, he would be happy with that.

Not so much.

"Why don't you ever wear lingerie?"

Ugh. Did this really need explaining? I'm overweight. I haven't had a thigh gap since first grade. My stomach looks like a topographical map of the Sierra Nevadas. Lingerie was only going to highlight the sad facts.

But I promised him I would try.

So I went out and bought some lingerie. But didn't want to put it on—I felt ridiculous. Like the fat girl in the movie who thinks she looks hot but whom everyone is secretly (or not so secretly) laughing at.

Several months after we were married, Roger and I were in a quaint little town in Northern California. Squeezed in between the shops of antique garden accessories and hand-made soaps was the cutest sleepwear boutique. All sorts of white cotton nightgowns and pajamas were in their front window. It was sweet and romantic, so Roger and I went inside to get me something lovely to sleep in.

Not lingerie, mind you. Sleepwear.

Once we found the perfect nightshirt, Roger pointed to a section in the back of the store that looked nothing like the grown-up Laura Ingalls fare that was in the front of the shop. This was definitely of a more "colorful" nature. We went through the racks. Finally, I came across a burgundy lace teddy.

"Yes. I'd really like to see you in that," Roger said.

"Really? I think I would look so fat in it." I hesitated.

"I think you would look really great."

For some reason, having Roger there assuring me he was looking forward to seeing me like that gave me the confidence to "suit up." I bought three different pieces of lingerie that day, and over the next week "revealed" a piece every couple of days.

Roger still counts that as one of the best weeks of his life.

A *Hot Mama* PLEDGE

I want our bedroom to be a sanctuary, so I will

- work to make our master bedroom a haven where intimacy thrives.
- set up the bedroom so that it's conducive to romance.
- invest time, energy, and money into making our master bedroom the retreat we need for our marriage to flourish.
- not allow romance-killers like laundry or bills to have permanent residence in our master bedroom.

REAL *Hot Mama* IDEAS

"I bought new sheets for our bed. Our old ones were ridiculous. They had butterflies on them. I'd had them since I was in high school. And for some reason, when we didn't get new sheets as a wedding gift, we decided they were good enough. They weren't. So today I splurged: I went to Bed Bath & Beyond and bought a brand-new set. They are navy blue and super soft. I spread them on our bed, and when my husband went to hop in, he stood back and grinned. Totally worth the money I spent."—Q

"I have gotten into the habit of taking a load of laundry out of the wash and putting it on my bed. And so many nights, my husband and I sweep the laundry off the bed and onto the floor where it sits as a reminder of all that I have to do. It doesn't exactly put me in the mood. So, today, I simply changed my habit. Instead of laying laundry on the bed, I put it on the couch. It turns out that out of sight, out of mind is a real thing. Good to know."—E

"I bought pink-tinged lightbulbs for our room. I read online that makes people look slimmer. At the very least, it made me feel more confident."—O

"I washed the bedding to make it smell nice, straightened up the bedroom, wore some perfume to bed, and . . . he didn't notice. I guess as long as ESPN is working, he doesn't care about that other stuff. But I noticed. And I was more into it, so that counts for something."—M

Hot Mama
"What Happens in the Bedroom" BUCKET LIST

1. Do one thing today that makes your bedroom sexier.

2. Change your sheets. You don't even have to get new ones. Clean ones make a huge difference.

3. Light a candle in your room when you go to bed.

4. Get new bed linens—especially if yours are old and ratty. (Note: men don't tend to love pink or hearts, so stick with nice, solid, manly colors or patterns lest your new bedding be a turnoff for him.)

5. Clean up your room. Put bills, laundry, and clutter away. Or at least move them to another room.

6. Change the lightbulbs in your room. Choose a soft light or soft color.

7. Ask your husband what makes him feel sexy in your bedroom. Make it happen.

Bonus Section

Ask Our Sexperts

Sex is one of those topics that inspires a lot of questions—and in Christian circles, those questions often go unanswered. That often leaves us feeling confused, ashamed, and unsure of what to do. So we asked a few sex experts—sexperts!—to help with some of the many questions posed to us while we worked on this book.

Our sexperts are men and women of integrity, professionals with master's degrees and doctorates in areas like psychotherapy and family counseling. Many are pastors or trained therapists. All follow Jesus. And none will skew the facts about sex to make you even more confused than you were before.

The questions in this section are real. They were sent to us by our readers through Facebook and email. We couldn't get an expert answer to every question that was sent to us, so we chose questions that seemed to come up again and again. We hope that by reading this you will not only get the answers you are seeking, but will also find camaraderie with like-minded Christian women. We're all in this together—and each of us feels a bit confused from time to time.

We hope these answers bring truth, honesty, and hope from true "sexperts" in a world where everything seems backward and truth seems hard to find.

Meet Our Sexperts

Jeff Hagen is a private practice OB/GYN physician with almost thirty years' experience treating women.

Rob Harrell is the senior pastor at Austin Oaks Church. He has a master of divinity from Southwestern Baptist Theological Seminary and a doctor of ministry from Dallas Theological Seminary.

Mike Kaylani has been married for fifteen years and has been blessed with two wonderful children. He has a master of divinity from Trinity Evangelical Divinity School and currently works at First Evangelical Free Church as a family and communities pastor.

Ginny Mosby is a licensed marriage and family therapist and a certified sex addiction therapist specializing in sexual trauma and recovery at Community Presbyterian Counseling Center in San Ramon, California.

Lucille Zimmerman is a licensed family counselor who practices in Littleton, Colorado, and the author of *Renewed: Finding Your Inner Happy in an Overwhelmed World*.

Happy reading!

Question: *My husband and I really don't seem to connect on a sexual level. Every time we have sex, it seems so awkward. We fumble around and try for a while but when it's over, I never feel satisfied. And I'm pretty sure he doesn't either. Are we just incompatible?—F*

Answer:

Dear F,

My experience as a wife and as a licensed professional counselor is that there are many doorways that lead us into connection with our partners. Once we enter one doorway, we can move around the house and open other doors. Imagine a guitar with several strings. Each string has an aspect of our humanness: physical, emotional, spiritual, sexual, psychological, and so on. We can pluck one string and the sound reverberates on the other strings.

Sex can be the same. Let's say I have a moment of deep spiritual connection with my husband in church. That spiritual longing and connectedness plucks our spiritual string but sometimes reverberates off our sexual string. Sometimes we can't wait to get home from church, if you know what I mean. Or maybe we take a long, hot hike together, and the sensation of being in tune with our physical string makes us consider being sexual.

Experts will tell you sex always starts in the brain. If you want to know more about this, I recommend Dr. Daniel Amen's book *Sex on the Brain*. If you want to make sex a priority and you don't feel that's happening on a physical level, then think of ways to bring the topic to your brain. For instance, some people get excited scheduling a time for sex on their calendar. That's because the brain starts anticipating and planning the event. Now, I might get people who disagree with me here, but since sex starts in the brain, I think it's okay to share fantasies with each other. Fantasies that you would never consider doing in real life. I would also explore other ways you could cause the brain to think about sex—for instance, using the five senses of sight, sound, smell, touch, and taste.

There could be many reasons you're not connecting on a sexual level. Our lives are busy with work, child rearing, and running to activities. If couples are overbooked or fighting, sexual intimacy is the first area that suffers. But with some work and intentionality, that "chemistry" that you are lacking can develop, and you'll find that the connection you don't think you have will grow.

—Lucille Zimmerman

Question: I'm not exactly "feeling it" when we have sex. It doesn't feel good to me so I sort of just smile and hope it will be over soon. My friend told me I should talk to my husband and tell him I'm not satisfied so he can try to make things better, but I'm scared to ask for what I want in bed. It feels so . . . uncomfortable. What can I do? Do you think it's wrong for a woman to, you know, ask for it?—O

Answer:

Dear O,

There is so much shame for Christians in the area of sex. On top of that, sex and intimacy are all about vulnerability. Those two things combined make it really hard to ask for what you want. It takes a lot of vulnerability. It's risky. Your partner could think you're a freak. I understand why you are scared.

But chances are your partner has things he wants as well, and he is also scared. If one person could take a risk—and I would suggest you start with something fairly safe—the other person will feel safer being able to say what they want. Of course, each person should feel free to say yes or no to any sexual activities. I've met with people in my counseling office who've done things with their partner that made them feel massive shame. No one should ever do something that makes them feel bad afterward.

My recommendation is to pick up a book by Christian authors who talk about this subject and read the book together (try Kevin Leman or Ed Wheat). You may not agree with everything they say in the book (I think you'll find that nobody has it all figured out) but use the book as a conversation starter. Part of the fun is continuing to grow and sort it out with your spouse.

—Lucille Zimmerman

....

Question: My husband and I have gotten so distant from each other! It's as if we're strangers living in the same house and whenever either of us talks to the other, we bark. I have to admit that sex is the last thing on my mind! How can I turn this around so we can have a connected marriage?—C

Answer:

Dear C,

I've taken a lot of training in Emotionally Focused Therapy (EFT) for marriage therapy. It was developed by the highly renowned psychologist Dr. Sue Johnson. The entire premise of the model is that our brains are wired to be deeply connected with our partner (this is all based on attachment theory) but sometimes partners struggle to be vulnerable with each other. Our society encourages independence and toughness, not vulnerability. It's hard for people to come home from a job where they've had to armor-up all day long and suddenly switch into the opposite mode. But vulnerability is what causes people to move toward one another.

I think God made our brains that way on purpose. Think about how quick your reaction is to someone who trips and falls. Unless you're a sociopath and incapable of empathy, you don't think about it . . . you rush toward the person to help them up. It's instinctual.

If one or both partners fear they are not as connected as they once were, internal alarm bells start to sound. But instead of using means that bring them close, they do things that push the other person farther away. Let me give you an example: If I ask my husband to spend time together and he turns to his computer to work, I wonder if he's not attracted to me anymore. Internally my alarms are sounding, so I harp on him: "You're always working. Why don't you spend time with me?" He doesn't say it, but inside he's thinking, *Darn, I can't make her happy. I'm not sure what to do, so I think I'll go to my computer where I'm successful at my job.* I get angrier, harp more, and he turns to his work to feel safe and have success. It destroys our connection.

Vulnerability is the key that changes this dynamic: If I say, "Honey, I'm scared. We haven't spent any time together for days. Are we still good?" my vulnerability doesn't threaten him. He can move toward that and comfort me: "Oh yes, I'm sorry, we need to plan a date." Now that's not as easy as it sounds. In fact, many people are so terrified of vulnerability that they need a therapist to help them change up their dance moves with one another.

—Lucille Zimmerman

* * *

Question: My husband is a withdrawer—he tends to keep his feelings stuffed inside and only talk when he feels it's absolutely necessary. This doesn't lend itself to very intimate conversations . . . especially on topics like sex. What can I do to help him feel comfortable to talk to me about tough topics?—M

Answer:

Dear M,

Men are socialized to keep vulnerable feelings to themselves, and your husband is probably no exception. When girls fall down, we pick them up and say something like, "Oh, honey! Are you okay?" We hug them and hold them until they are done crying, and we wipe their tears with affection. When boys fall down, we are more likely to say something like, "Get up and brush it off! You're okay!" When they continue to cry we often tell them to stop their crying. Messages to "suck it up," "take it like a man," and "don't cry like a girl" are pervasive throughout a boy's growing up years from parents, coaches, and peers.

What a blessing that God puts us together, man and woman—for so many reasons! One of them is that as women we have the opportunity to help our men be more connected to the emotional part of themselves they were trained to turn off. But this kind of emotional intimacy requires both vulnerability and safety. In order to be vulnerable, we need to be in an emotionally safe environment. When we ask our husbands to share their feelings, we need to take a good look at our own ability to be emotionally safe enough for them to do so.

Ask yourself some questions and be honest with yourself. Am I able to hear my husband share feelings without minimizing them or trying to talk him out of the feelings? Am I able to allow him to feel hurt, sad, or confused without getting defensive or critical? Am I able to be genuinely curious and ask questions so that I can fully understand his emotional experience, even if it is very different from how I would feel in a similar situation? Be open to asking him if there is anything you do that makes him feel unsafe when he shares his feelings.

Practice these skills in everyday conversations about feelings. As you are able to provide safety when he is vulnerable, the emotional intimacy will increase. Remember that talk about sex is probably the most emotionally vulnerable topic we venture into as a couple.

If you are able to be safe, and he says he feels safe but still is not able to be vulnerable, there may be a deep emotional wound that needs healing. Meeting with a pastor, couples mentor, or therapist can help you work through these obstacles.

—Ginny Mosby

Question: I have three kids under five, and honestly, the last thing I want after a long day is for my husband to touch me. Okay, maybe he can give me a massage, but that's it. Still, I want our marriage to be strong. What can I do to get myself in the mood?—G

Answer:

Dear G,

This is a very common challenge for couples who have very young children. It can be a difficult transition to shift from Mommy to Lover. With kids constantly pulling at you for attention and physical care, it is very easy to become neglectful of your own needs. Then

Hubby comes home and he wants your attention too, and you are out of gas.

Healthy sexuality is about more than just sex; it's about self-identity, relationship, partnership, emotional connection, and more. How do you see yourself? Have you become so immersed in your role as mother that you have lost touch with your own needs, interests, and passions? Have you sacrificed self-care for parenting? A positive self-perception that includes embracing your sexual self and empowers you to express needs is key to a healthy sex life with your husband. If you think of making love as "for him," that may be an indicator that you have lost touch with your needs as well as your sexual self.

On a practical level, involve your husband in the evening and weekend routines with the children. Experiencing him as an equal parenting partner may just turn you on to him as a lover. Additionally, an extra pair of hands getting things done may leave more time for relaxing together and just enjoying one another, opening the door to embracing your sexual self and more sexy time with your husband.

If you are able to make time for self-care and are finding time to connect with your husband but you still have no sexual desire, check with your doctor. Rule out any medical issues that might be affecting your own sexual desire. Testosterone levels in both men and women affect sex drive, arousal, and release. If your levels are low, this could be impacting your interest in sexual intimacy with your husband.

—Ginny Mosby

Question: *I keep reading about how sex should be mutu-*
ally fulfilling and how each partner should care about
the other's physical enjoyment as well as emotional
enjoyment. But my husband isn't like that at all! He
seems to think sex is just for him, which means as soon
as he is finished, sex is over. It's very frustrating, to say
the least. Plus, it really hurts my feelings. I feel like he
doesn't love me because he doesn't seem to care about
my enjoyment. What can I do?—H

Answer:

Dear H,

The first step is to have some conversations about
your sex life together. Tell him the ways you enjoy your
sexual intimacy and then share some ways you would
like to see your sex life improve. Ask him to share the
same with you about his experience of your sex life.

He may not understand the sexual arousal and release
cycle for you as a woman since it is different from the
way men experience sexual arousal and release. A good
book to read together to broaden your knowledge of
your sexuality and sexual intimacy in your relationship
is *The Gift of Sex* by Penner and Penner.

If it feels like he is disconnected from you during sex,
try having sex with the lights on and your eyes open to
maintain the connection with one another.

Also, I don't want to overstep, but this question raises
concerns for me about whether there is something else
going on in your sex life. The impact of porn and sex

addiction on sexual intimacy in marriage often results in this kind of experience for partners . . . the lack of connection and mutuality in the intimacy.

In my counseling practice, I am seeing more and more men and women getting pulled into the abyss of online pornography. The average age of exposure is eleven years old!

One of my colleagues does a lot of work with teens and volunteers in youth ministry in her church. Several months ago, she got a small group of guys to be willing to be open with her, and she asked them about their experiences and beliefs about sex and pornography. They told her that "all" guys view pornography and the only difference between Christians and non-Christians is that the Christians are "struggling" with it.

When she asked a group of girls about sex, they said they believe the guys are all viewing porn as well and that they have to perform in order to be in a relationship. When she asked them what they thought God's design for healthy sexuality was, they said they had no idea other than sex was not okay before marriage.

The messages communicated through pornography are quite the opposite of the truth of God-designed healthy sexuality. Porn-related sex involves using someone, and is performance-oriented, separate from love, emotionally distant, and for impulse gratification. Healthy sexuality includes caring for someone, sharing with a partner, an expression of love, emotional closeness, and lasting gratification.

All that to say, if you are concerned that your husband is involved in pornography or some other sort of sexual addiction, I encourage you to seek help from a counselor or your pastor.

—Ginny Mosby

....

Question: *Ever since I had my baby, sex has been . . . well, it's been painful. I feel so dry down there. Is there something I can do to get things back to normal?—T*

Answer:

Dear T,

First of all, don't be alarmed. Many, many women struggle with dryness after childbirth. This has to do with a lot of factors—hormones and biological changes, and even the fact that you don't have sex for six weeks after you have the baby so your body's natural lubrication diminishes.

I would try an over-the-counter lubricant first—something as simple as KY Jelly can make a big difference. Try it for a few days. If that doesn't do the trick, I would call your OB and have him or her check you. If there is no bigger issue (sometimes an infection can cause pain during sex), then this sort of thing can be treated with a prescription cream or even some tablets.

But I also want to remind you that time will help you heal. Your body went through some trauma and will take a bit of time to get back to normal. Plus, as I said above, the more sex you have, the more natural lubricant your body will make, so having sex more often will probably help you want to have sex more often.

—Jeff Hagen

• •

Question: I have a much stronger sex drive than my husband. I want it every night and he always seems to fake a headache. Is there something wrong with me? Is it normal that I want him more than he wants me?—K

Answer:

Dear K,

Whenever I hear that question in my office (or the opposite question—that a husband wants his wife more than she wants him), I always have the same answer: there is nothing wrong with you or your husband. The only thing wrong is that you have different sex drives. There is no "normal" here, and sometimes two people just don't have the same drive. And that's okay.

If you think about the situation and realize that he does want to have sex with you—and often—but just not as often as you want to have sex with him, then I would venture that you both have normal, adult sex drives and yours is just a bit higher than his.

That said, with men, a low sex drive is almost always physiological. Male sex drive hinges on testosterone levels, and thus, if a man is struggling with libido, there is often a much simpler fix than if there is a struggle with a woman. See if he would be willing to see a counselor or his physician, because something as simple as an antidepressant or a testosterone supplement could make a big difference.

On the flip side, a woman's sex drive is much more complicated than a man's. It involves so many factors—physiological, yes, but also emotional, genetic, hereditary, and even cyclical. If you give a woman a testosterone supplement, it hardly addresses issues with sex drive, as it's only a small player in all of the pieces that make up her sex drive. But, that doesn't seem to be your problem.

In short, my answer is that no, nothing is wrong with you. But if you feel concerned, you should talk to your doctor or encourage your husband to talk to his, because sometimes things can be done to resolve the issue.

I hope that helps.

—Jeff Hagen

Question: *Is there anything that's off-limits morally or biblically sex-wise between two married, Christian adults?—U*

Answer:

Dear U,

In Hebrews 13:4, the Bible says, "Marriage should be honored by all, and the marriage bed kept pure, for God will judge the adulterer and all the sexually immoral." First Corinthians 7:1–5 says:

> Now for the matters you wrote about: "It is good for a man not to have sexual relations with a woman."

But since sexual immorality is occurring, each man should have sexual relations with his own wife, and each woman with her own husband. The husband should fulfill his marital duty to his wife, and likewise the wife to her husband. The wife does not have authority over her own body but yields it to her husband. In the same way, the husband does not have authority over his own body but yields it to his wife. Do not deprive each other except perhaps by mutual consent and for a time, so that you may devote yourselves to prayer. Then come together again so that Satan will not tempt you because of your lack of self-control.

These two passages tell us that sexual intimacy is a gift from God to be enjoyed in a covenant relationship called marriage. The man and woman are not to deprive one another of intimacy, except when there are spiritual reasons for doing so. And ultimately, a married couple should seek to serve one another's intimacy needs, seeking to give joy to the other and not primarily seeking their own pleasure.

Practically, when this occurs, there is great joy in serving the needs of the other. That said, there should always be regard for what each feels is appropriate and comfortable for the other, because that's an expression of true love and humility—not looking to one's own interests, but to the interests of others (see Phil. 2:1–5).

So, to answer your question, have honest dialogue and discussion with your spouse so that you can understand how he or she feels about what is appropriate and pleasing. Within those bounds, I think anything is acceptable.

—Rob Harrell

. . . .

Question: Is it okay to use sex toys with my husband?—N

Answer:

Dear N,

I would say that I am not qualified to answer this question for lack of personal knowledge regarding the realm of sex toys. I do know that sex was meant to be enjoyed between a husband and wife, and thus I would have a hard time condemning something that both of you enjoyed using—the key being that both of you enjoy it.

With that said, my one concern is that sex toys or games can border on the realm of fantasy. By definition, fantasy is a break from reality, and I believe that God wants us to enjoy sex in reality with the partner he has given to us. Fantasy opens up a world where people think there are no consequences when there always are, especially when it comes to our sexual desires. Ultimately, every husband and every wife wants to be sexually appealing to their spouse for who they are. Fantasy can send the opposite message.

—Mike Kaylani

Question: *My adult young married Sunday school class at church is doing a series on sex and I'm completely baffled. I always assumed sex and church don't mix, but I also feel like I sometimes get mixed messages as Christian books (and the Bible!) say sex is an essential, godly part of marriage. Should we be talking about sex at church?—L*

Answer:

Dear L,

Feel free to follow your conscience on this matter.

For some, speaking about intimacy is a very private matter. No one should feel any need to bring themselves to a place of discomfort . . . especially in an adult fellowship class. And if the conversation is making you feel uncomfortable—or worse, if you think it's unbiblical—then I suggest you speak with church leadership about it.

That said, God is the Creator of human beings, whom he joyfully made to be sexual. He could have made sexual intimacy in marriage a matter of "utility"—simply for the procreation of the human race. But because of his grace and kindness, he made sex pleasurable for humans. Without a doubt, that reveals something about the character and purposes of God. And while the Bible does not speak in detail about the joy of sexual intimacy (except in Song of Solomon), it does speak about the fulfillment found in intimacy in the midst of covenant relational commitment found in marriage. And I believe that in the context of healthy, adult relationships, that can be discussed in a mature and helpful fashion in the context of church.

—Rob Harrell

· ·

Question: I'm just going to come out and say it: I think I've fallen in love. I met O at work and we had an instant chemistry. As I've gotten to know him, I've found him to be kind and honest and funny. And he genuinely cares about me. My husband is just the opposite. He's caught up in his work, he is gruff, and he never asks me about my day. I feel so lonely in my marriage. I admit I'm tempted to just end things with my husband and start over with O. Is that so wrong? Wouldn't God want me to be happy?—T

Answer:

Dear T,

As a pastor, my first temptation is to give you a list of verses (like Eph. 5:6, 2 Tim. 2:22, or 1 Thess. 4:4) that show the Bible's take on sexual sin. But seeing as how your question shows clear trepidation, I can assume you know what is right and wrong in God's eyes. With that in mind, I think what you are really asking me is to tell you how to overcome this temptation.

Sexual sin is tempting—the grass always looks greener there and it's easy to get swept away in one moment. But that one moment has great consequences. And while every one of us has weakness and a tendency

153

to fall into sin, only by sticking to what we know is good, true, and right can we honor God.

I tell my congregants that there are five steps to sinking into the temptation of sexual sin:

Step 1: Desensitization. You begin to wonder if our culture got it right about sex and marriage and God got it wrong. You start looking elsewhere for your joy instead of to God.

Step 2: Relaxation. You relax your standards a little bit. You flirt. You go to lunch with your friend O.

Step 3: Fixation. You think about O constantly. You think about how handsome he is. You imagine your life with him instead of with your husband.

Step 4: Rationalization. You rationalize. Why wouldn't God want you to be happy? Why should you stick it out with your husband when he doesn't give you what you need?

Step 5: Degeneration. You act on your desires.

After reading your question, I'd guess you are on step 4, walking quickly toward step 5. That is a scary place to be! And I'm glad you decided to ask this question before taking that final step. It shows me that it's not too late for you to turn this around and get the help you need.

It is possible to stop this train on the tracks before anything more happens. God always provides a way to walk away from any temptation. You have taken four steps toward the temptation of sexual sin. Now it's time to start walking in the other direction. And here are some powerful, daily steps that can help you walk away from it:

Step 1: Refuse to rationalize. Push thoughts like "If only you knew my husband" or "O truly loves me" out of your mind.

Step 2: Bring it into the light. I know it's hard to share sin with others, but only by bringing this temptation into the open with a trusted friend or counselor can you begin to walk away from it.

Step 3: Become accountable. I often tell people to share the last 10 percent—those thoughts and feelings that you don't think you can share with anyone. Only through sharing the struggle can you begin to move past it.

Step 4: Maximize the benefits and minimize the lure. Remind yourself often of the benefits of your self-control (e.g., you honor God, your finances stay stable, your kids stay in a loving home) and minimize the lure (e.g., your family and life will be torn apart by an affair).

Step 5: Seek truth. Search your Bible for Scripture on morality, on honesty, on truth. Read these verses often.

Step 6: Carefully analyze who your actions would hurt. Think about the people involved in the decisions you are making. Your kids. Your spouse. O's family. Your extended family.

Step 7: Turn your energy to your spouse. As painful as your marriage is right now, one of the best things you can do is focus your sexual energy on your spouse, the one you made a covenant to love.

Step 8: Repent. Prayerfully and earnestly repent of your actions.

Follow these steps every day until you feel the temptation fade—and I assure you, if you focus your eyes on

Jesus, it will fade. In its place, you'll find hope, grace, and the joy that only comes from walking closely with him.

—Rob Harrell

* * *

Question: I think my husband is having an affair. He keeps coming home late from work, and then last night, I saw a text message on his phone from H that said, "See you tomorrow at 5. Can't wait." I asked him about it and he snapped at me not to read his messages. What should I do? I want to honor my marriage vows, but he doesn't seem to be.—W

Answer:

Dear W,

You have every right to be concerned by his behavior, although I wouldn't assume the worst without clear knowledge. It sounds like each of you is feeling unloved by the other. Whether he is having an affair or not, your relationship is not where it ought to be.

My first suggestion would be to ask God for strength to love him for better or for worse. That doesn't mean enabling or accepting his behavior, but it does mean showing him respect in how you confront him. You need to be able to clearly tell him that you have concerns in a way that shows him that you are hoping for the best for both of you. If (and only if) he refuses to talk openly with you about your concerns and feelings, then I would solicit the aid of a male friend he respects, asking that person to talk to him about what he won't discuss with you. Regardless, I would go to your church for help.

Whatever happens, seek help from a loving Christian friend, a Christian counselor, or your church. You need support right now.

—Mike Kaylani

Question: I didn't become a Christian until I was forty. Because of this, I have a very sordid past and I have had sex with more than twenty men. My husband also didn't become a Christian until later in life, and he also had a colorful sexual past. We both have repented. And we both want to stay faithful to God's plan for our marriage. But, honestly, it's really hard to just forget about all of those past experiences. Sometimes when we're having sex, I think about them. And often when we're not having sex, I feel guilty about them. What can I do?—S

Answer:

Dear S,

Know that you are a new creation in Christ; the old is GONE! What you have with your husband now is not the same as what you had in your past. Yes, the physical act may have been the same, but your sex life is so much more than that now. It is vital to not equate your past sexual experiences with your present. You can carry forward an attitude of shame that will diminish the beauty and pleasure God intended sex to give to you and your husband. You need to proclaim freedom from old shame and embrace the gift you now have.

It is my prayer that you and your husband would explore the fullness of sex as God intended and let that growing understanding crowd out the memories of old. You may not be able to forget those things, but you can replace them with something better. Reading a book like this or some others that speak of the gift of sex together as a couple and allowing them to fuel your own sex life will help you move on to a new level of understanding and satisfaction.

—Mike Kaylani

Girlfriend-to-Girlfriend Q&A

There are some questions that you need a girlfriend to answer. And when it comes to things like what shade of lipstick to wear on date night and what music to blast in your car, you probably have countless girlfriends to ask. But when it comes to those super private (and yes, sometimes embarrassing) questions about sex, it's harder to find someone to ask.

Enter our girlfriend panel: fun, sexy hot mamas just like you who have the real, tried-and-true answers to all of your sex questions. These women may not have fancy titles behind their names, but they certainly have the experience, passion, and loving relationships to prove that they really know what they are talking about.

Meet Our Girlfriends

Bonny Logsdon Burns is the woman behind Pearl's Oyster Bed7 (www.OysterBed7.com), a blog written to encourage low-libido wives through a Christian lens. She is currently completing her study to become a Christian counselor.

Jay Dee is a sex educator and the founder of the blog www. sexwithinmarriage.com. Admittedly, he is a man, and thus can't be a girlfriend, but we thought his advice qualified him to write for this section. Plus, it's kind of nice to get a man's perspective, isn't it?

Kathi Lipp. You already know Kathi, but she wanted to lend some thoughts to this section and, well, she's pretty much the ultimate girlfriend.

Cheryl McKay is the screenwriter of *The Ultimate Gift* and coauthor of *Never the Bride*. She and her husband, Chris, have a marriage ministry called Finally One (www.finallyone.com) and are currently producing a video series called *Married with Benefits*.

Diandra Phillips is a married mom of three who lives in Texas. She serves as a MOPS steering committee leader and works part-time for her church.

....

Question: The idea of my husband touching me after I've been touched all day definitely sends me searching for those flannel pajamas. What can I do to get myself in the mood?—I

Answer:

Dear I,

I totally understand this question! I've found that getting healthy has helped my physical craving for sex. In spite of hating to sweat, I've experienced the joys of consistent exercise. I've found that better eating habits help me feel sexier because I lose the gross full and bloated feeling. Bloodwork revealed some things my body lacked, so I started taking supplements and bio-identical hormones. However, to be honest, getting healthy only upped my hot quotient by about 25 percent.

I've come to realize that I'm a high-drive spouse when it comes to desiring emotional and spiritual connection. The physical lags behind, but it catches up once we get frisky with foreplay. There are studies that prove some women fire up after things begin.

My answer to your question: you just decide to "get busy." Decide to be sexual with your husband for the benefit of your marriage in spite of having inconsistent or nonexistent physical sexual cravings.

You may not feel a yearning deep inside before the next rendezvous, but you will remember how luscious you felt during the last one and how close you felt after it. That will spur you on to more frequent encounters. I've found, and again studies have proven, that the more you have sex the more you'll physically want to have sex.

A couple of other things to consider regarding low libido are what medications you are taking and if you have had sexual trauma in your past. Hormonal birth control and SSRI antidepressants are notorious for dampening sex drive. Speak with your physician about possible substitutions that are still effective. If you are having trouble finding resolution from past sexual abuse or premarital sexual experiences, seek help from a Christian counselor who specializes in sexual issues.

—Bonny Logsdon Burns

....

Question: I want to have more sex. And better sex. What are some easy things I can do to make sure our sex life is frequent and fantastic?—B

Answer:

Dear B,

This is actually a difficult question to answer, because the solution is based largely on the context of your own marriage. I'm going to work with the following assumption: you are married, a woman, and have a lower sex drive than your husband. I'm using these parameters because I believe they will fit the majority of the readers of this book.

Now, everyone wants easy answers, quick tips, or a series of steps to guarantee an outcome. But unfortunately, real life doesn't work that way. There are no easy answers. Instead, we have simple answers that take a lifetime to learn to apply. These simple answers may by no means be easy, but I think they have a far higher chance of working in the long run. You don't want to have a brief fling with a new activity or position and then get bored and be back at square one.

So, how do you have more and better sex?

First, make sex a priority in your marriage. Simple, right? But how do we do that? Making sex a priority in your marriage means being intentional about having sex. It means making time for sex, and that may mean actually scheduling sex in advance. For those who feel like scheduling sex would be unromantic, or unexciting, tell me how long in advance you scheduled your wedding. Was it romantic? Did you wake up on the morning of your wedding day just bursting in anticipation? Scheduled sex can be romantic and exciting, the same as spontaneous sex. What planning does is remove the constant anxiety of "Are we going to have sex tonight?" And if you know your husband realizes you're going to have sex, regardless of his actions, then you can stop thinking of his affectionate gestures as an attempt to get sex. It also helps you think ahead toward sex, which might help your sex drive warm up throughout the day.

Making sex a priority also means giving up other activities for sex—it means sacrificing for sex. What takes up your nights now? TV? Movies? Social media? Games on your computer, phone, or tablet? Imagine how much sex you could have if you gave that up. What if you fasted from these things for a week? What if you had sex every night for a week instead? Think it's impossible? Try it. Your marriage will never be the same.

But, what about making sex better? Again, there are two simple—but not easy—answers. The first is to relax your boundaries a bit. Now, I don't mean good, biblical, moral boundaries—there are reasons God asks us not to do certain things. But I know that some people have set up boundaries around sex to make themselves more comfortable—and comfort almost always excludes excitement. For something to be exciting it has to be a bit dangerous, a bit new (or at least not mundane).

Second, to make sex better, you're going to have to step a little outside of your comfort zone. What are your boundaries? Do you only have sex with the lights off? Only at night? Only in bed? Only in one position? Think about the range of sexual activities you can explore with your spouse. Are there some that you have been shying away from because they make you uncomfortable? I know there will be readers who have never touched their husband's body except for the parts that come into contact during sex in the missionary position, and then only in the dark. Explore the possibilities, explore your husband, and explore yourself, together. I know, it's scary, but you didn't want safe, you wanted exciting. Not sure what the possibilities are? Then start reading.

Fair warning: you have to be careful with what you read, as some of the sex advice you will find on the internet is not good, godly counsel. That said, there are many Christian marriage bloggers out there who can give you some ideas for your marriage. On my blog (www.sexwithinmarriage.com), I answer a lot of questions from readers, and in doing so, I explore quite a few of these activities. The Christian Marriage Bloggers Association (www.upliftingmarriage.com) has about a hundred Christian bloggers—a library's worth of posts on the subject of marriage and sex from a Christian perspective. Start reading.

Lastly, what ultimately makes sex better and more exciting is more intimacy. This can only be gained through time—intentional time. Intimacy affects every part of your marriage. Increase your physical intimacy by having more and varied sex. Increase your emotional intimacy by talking more, and about things that matter to both of you. Talk about the scary stuff: your hopes, dreams, fears, desires, and goals. Want to get really intimate? Start talking about sex! Build spiritual intimacy by talking about your beliefs, going to church together, reading your Bible together, studying God's Word together. Can you guess what will bring you closer than ever? Pray about sex together! Again, these are simple things, but they're not easy. Intimacy requires vulnerability, and vulnerability is scary! You think it's frightening to be seen naked in the light? I'm telling you, your husband is likely more scared to have his emotions or his daily fears shown in the light.

It takes time to get to the level where you can share these things comfortably. So you're going to have to start doing it when it's uncomfortable, when it's not safe, because after all, you want adventure, and adventure starts with taking a risk. So take that first step, and see how good it can get.

—Jay Dee

Question: *My husband and I stayed pure before we got married—we even waited to kiss until our wedding night. I always thought because we "did it right" that God would bless us with an amazing sex life. But instead, it's really awkward. I really don't want to have*

*sex at all most days because it's just so emotionally
exhausting. What are we doing wrong?—Q*

Answer:

Dear Q,

First, I want to say, what an awesome thing it is you
both waited. We should never regret doing things God's
way, even if things don't go as well as we'd hoped. You
do have the rest of your lives to figure this out together
and don't have to get it right from the beginning.

I think every couple goes through some degree of
struggle in the "getting to know each other" phase,
especially if sex is brand-new. But what I have found is
that with time it's gotten so much better. One of the
main reasons for that is my husband and I have a very
communicative relationship about sex. We are not embarrassed to talk about it in and out of the bedroom.
During non-intimate times, we may tease about what's
to come or mention a fun memory from the night before. It's not a "hidden topic" that only comes out when
it's "go time." Having this open communication un-
dercuts the embarrassment or awkwardness that could
inhibit us. So, a great first step may be ratcheting up
your communication. Don't be afraid to discuss what
works, what doesn't, what you want to try, what you
don't, what frustrates each of you. Once you start to
enjoy things, be very open about that too.

We also try to keep a healthy sense of humor about
the fun, the foibles, the successes, the near misses, or
what can feel like downright failures. Our motto is

"Naked and unashamed"—keeping that sense of "This is God's gift for us to enjoy, and we don't have to be shy about it." That has really helped break down the barriers to sex that can get somewhat awkward. If you can find your sense of humor—whether things go well and especially if they don't—it definitely helps. If you focus on what's gone wrong in the past or what's been awkward, you will stay tense—even fearful—about returning to the conversation . . . or to the bedroom.

Besides communication and humor, I think it would help you if you first focus on building good, intimate memories together. Without those, it's hard to encourage yourselves back into the bedroom—or the kitchen or the living room floor—or wherever you'd like to get creative. This may take baby steps at first. It may not take you all the way to intercourse. But you need non-pressurized, fun and playful sexual times together so you aren't only remembering the frustration that creates anxiety and puts pressure on you both. A lack of good memories will only encourage you to stay away from the bedroom. But staying out of that room is going to damage your marriage.

You can start small. For example, have a make-out session with no intention of moving toward sex. Give each other a sensual massage. Take the time to make the environment romantic. Since you, as a woman, especially know what you need in those moments to relax, set the scene yourself. Don't be afraid to take the lead on that because your husband can't read your mind. Or be very clear about what you'd like his role to be in setting up the romance. You can take turns with this, bringing new ideas to the table for settings and atmosphere, music, positions, and so on. Take your time and don't be in a rush. Make sure you carve out time for this when you're not ridiculously tired at the end of a long day. (It's extremely hard to get turned on at that time, and if you aren't turned on, it will be awkward or painful, creating more bad memories.) Pick times that you know you'll be at your best. You two deserve the best of each other, not the leftovers. For example, if you don't do well on a full stomach, plan your rendezvous before dinner and let dinner be the dessert. If you don't do well at night after a long day, plan a time for the morning. Don't be afraid to try something new and fail. It's better than not trying at all.

The more good memories you build, the more you'll want to build, which will strengthen your bond and your marriage.

—Cheryl McKay

· ·

Question: *If it were up to my husband, we'd have sex every night. If it were up to me, we'd have sex once a month. What's the happy medium?—N*

Answer:

Dear N,

Figuring out why you only want to have sex once a month is half the battle. Are you feeling that you should only have sex with him when he "deserves" it and he rarely deserves it? Or are you truly just not physically motivated? Neither scenario has to be a permanent situation. Marital conflict can be solved and resources are out there to give you ideas of how to ramp up your physical sex drive. It is possible to work on both issues at the same time. Actually, working on sex will speed up solving the other problems!

You and your husband have to talk this one out. Part of satisfaction in the bedroom is being able to have a conversation about sex outside of the bedroom. Whatever the problem may be, desire discrepancy or insensitive lovemaking, the best time to talk about this is in neutral territory (like over a cup of coffee at the kitchen counter).

Figuring out a happy compromise regarding frequency is an important conversation. Start the discussion knowing that every night is too much and once a month is too little.

Generally, couples have sex 2–3 times a week. However, 25 percent of women are the spouse with the higher sex drive and would love to have sex every day. They have often told me that I should be grateful to have a husband who desires me often. Knowing that, I've been humbled to realize having a husband want you every night isn't a bad situation to be in.

—Bonny Logsdon Burns

Question: *It seems like the more I have sex, the more I want sex. Why is that?*—C

Answer:

Dear C,

There are quite a few things working together physiologically and emotionally to make this occur.

When you have sex, there are changes in your body. When you have sex, your brain is flooded with the hormone oxytocin, which is called the "love hormone" or the "bonding hormone." It is a chemical produced by our brains to make us bond, to fall in love. Men are generally in very short supply of this chemical. Guess when we get the largest dose. That's right, at the time of orgasm. At that moment, we generally have seven times the levels of oxytocin in our body as usual . . . for about half an hour. (Quick tip: if you can get your guy to talk instead of fall asleep during this half hour, you are likely to have a much more emotionally intimate conversation than at any other time. Some men get really talkative during this period, because oxytocin makes them feel safe and secure. Good to know, right?)

Also, if you are having unprotected sex, then there is a transmission of semen, which includes a small dose of testosterone that your body will absorb. It's perfectly harmless, and women have testosterone in their bodies, it's just at much lower levels than men. In fact, it's so low in comparison that this injection of new testosterone may temporarily increase sexual drive.

In addition to this, sex is exercise. The more active you are during sex (which I highly recommend), the more exercise you get. Exercise does a great many things for your body, not the least of which is to increase sexual drive. It also increases blood flow, which makes you more sexually responsive. To add to that, you also get a nice burst of hormones in your system: oxytocin (mentioned above) and dopamine. Dopamine is a "reward" hormone. You get doses of this whenever you do something new and exciting, and it's highly addictive. So, the more often you have sex, the more dopamine you get—causing you to want more sex.

Sex causes emotional changes too. Have you ever noticed that your husband gets grumpy after a week or two of not having sex? Why? Well, there are a couple of reasons. For one, men feel a physical pressure for sexual release that can become painful. Also, a lot of a man's emotional security is wrapped up in his sex life. If we don't have sex, we don't feel secure, we don't feel loved . . . and that's scary. But we're not allowed to be scared, so we get grumpy. So when your husband gets grumpy because you haven't had sex, try to remember that it's his way of saying he misses you and is worried you don't love him anymore. Remember, he has one-seventh of the oxytocin that you do. He feels abandoned and unloved a lot quicker than you do without that oxytocin. Hugs and kisses will help the oxytocin a bit, but dragging him off to bed is a lot more effective, for both of you.

Back to the point. After sex, both you and your husband will feel more safe, secure, loving, and loved. You are more likely to show affection, to open up, to talk and share. This in turn improves your relationship, which again increases your desire for him.

So as you can see, it's a few things working together that cause you to want more sex when you have more sex. But, here's the problem. It works in reverse as well. What happens if you don't have sex frequently?

Well, your body gets used to not having dopamine and forgets that sex makes it feel good. Your oxytocin levels stay at normal, which means you and your husband have to work harder to feel connected and bonded. Your husband gets grumpier and grumpier, causing your relationship to be rockier and rockier. Eventually, you distance yourselves because it's uncomfortable to be that close to someone physically without being close emotionally. And then it gets dangerous. Because you aren't only missing sex, you are missing intimacy—on all levels—and then other people start looking like viable sources for intimacy. After all, most affairs are not about sex, they are about intimacy. I believe this is why Paul wrote,

> Do not deprive each other of sexual relations, unless you both agree to refrain from sexual intimacy for a limited time so you can give yourselves more completely to prayer. Afterward, you should come together again so that Satan won't be able to tempt you because of your lack of self-control. (1 Corinthians 7:5 NLT)

It is dangerous to go too long without sex in a marriage. Luckily there is an easy cure: go have sex. If I just described your marriage, put down this book and go now. If your husband asks, "What's gotten into you?" you can just tell him your Bible told you to have more sex . . . Watch his respect for the Bible go up a notch.

I believe God created this system, and I believe God designed us to have regular, even frequent, sex in marriage. When Paul wrote this verse, the assumption of the rabbis at the time was that a woman whose husband came home every night should be having sex daily, and that the longest you could fast from sex by law was a week, during a woman's menses. What if you had sex every night for a week? Willing to find out what it would do for your marriage?

—Jay Dee

Question: *I waited to have sex until I was married and couldn't wait to finally be intimate with my beloved groom. But my fantasy came crashing to a halt the first time we had sex . . . It was far from pleasurable. In fact, it hurt. I kept trying, but things haven't seemed to improve, and I'm to the point where the mere mention of having sex makes me want to run and hide. I want to give myself to my husband, but I can't tolerate the pain. I'm so frustrated, and while my husband is understanding, I'm sure he's frustrated too. What can I do?—E*

Answer:

Dear E,

Before we were married, my husband and I both thought sex was going to be awesome . . . It wasn't. It hurt so badly! We thought we'd spend our whole honeymoon having sex, but instead we spent our whole honeymoon with me crying about how much I hated having sex. It was so frustrating and disappointing. I was embarrassed and felt really bad for my husband.

I finally called my OB to see what the problem was, and I'm so glad I did. She gave me some numbing ointment that she said wouldn't take away all of the feeling but would make sex less painful. And it worked! I just had to put a little bit of it on before we had sex and we were good to go.

Sex got better and better, and eventually, I was able to stop using the ointment. But then I had my first baby, and six weeks postpartum, I learned the hard way that it was once again painful to have sex. I went back to my OB. She did a quick check and discovered a lot of scar tissue from my episiotomy. At that point, my choices were to have a procedure done to repair the scar tissue or start using the numbing ointment until I was done having babies. I used the ointment for a few years and then had my OB repair the area when I was done having babies.

My point is, I understand how frustrating it is to have pain with sex. And while it's embarrassing, the first thing you need to do is call your OB and schedule an appointment. Tell her what is going on and have her examine you. I remember thinking that I must be the only woman in the world dealing with this sort of thing, but my OB assured me that it's very normal. And that she had a whole bunch of tricks to help make things better.

So get help. Your sex life is worth it!

—Diandra Phillips

Question: My husband complained to me the other day that I never want to have sex with him. When I think

*about it, he's right. I'm never really in the mood and
so I just say no. Is that so wrong?*—C

Answer:

Dear C,

Before I started reclaiming my libido, I often wondered
why sex was necessary. What I didn't understand as a low-
drive wife is that my husband connects emotionally with
me through sex. It's not just a physical act; it's a symbol
of love to him. I thought he was clawing at me just to
have physical release. But that just wasn't true. So when
I denied him, what he heard was, "I don't love you." Why
doesn't your husband just tell you this? He may not realize
how to verbalize it to you—especially if he is frustrated.

Is it so wrong? Well, I've found that God created sexual
intimacy to be the glue of marriage. Sexual intimacy is
what sets marriage apart from all other relationships. Do
you really want to just be roommates with your husband?
Why did you get married if this is what it boils down to?

Sex biochemically and spiritually bonds husbands
and wives. When we have sex, our brains are flooded
with oxytocin. During orgasm, practically oceans full
of oxytocin are released (even without orgasm, it's still
buckets full). Oxytocin is the relational bonding chemical in our brains. Sex also enables us to bond spiritually,
and how this happens is God's mystery. But I'm here to
testify as a low-libido wife that having consistent sexual
intimacy draws you closer to each other in a way only
God can do. What wife doesn't want to feel emotionally
and spiritually connected with her husband?

In 1 Corinthians 7, Paul suggests (it's not a command) married couples not deprive one another so that temptation doesn't sneak in. A lot of people like to use this passage as a weapon against wives who refuse sexual relations. But I think wives would be less likely to refuse if they were shown God's plan. God created our bodies. He designed sexual intimacy to exude spiritual, emotional, and physical benefits for both husband and wife. Even if a wife has no sex drive, she still benefits from sexual intimacy!

When I rejected sex with my husband, I was rejecting the emotional connection I most craved, and in a way I was rejecting God's plan. To have the most potential for an incredible marriage, learn why you are never "in the mood" and take steps to fix it. Low libido can result from relational problems as well as physical problems. Low libido is not a permanent condition and neither are problems in your marriage. Don't know where to start? Start where I did: in prayer. God will show you the way to improved marital intimacy.

—Bonny Logsdon Burns

Question: My husband struggles with impotence. What can I do to help him?—S

Answer:

Dear S,

Here are a few things I would recommend to anyone who is married to a man who is struggling with impotence.

1. Get your doctor involved. There are so many more options available to men these days than even ten years ago. Your husband may need to take medication, but it's likely he won't need to take it all the time. The meds can cause headaches and make everything look a bit hazy. But headaches and looking at the world through Barney-colored glasses is well worth it.

2. Realize it has zero to do with you. (Zero!) Many wives feel that it must be that their husbands have lost interest in them or don't find them sexually attractive anymore. But this is a physical issue that happens to most men eventually. If you felt like skipping this section because it's not a problem in your marriage, realize that eventually, it probably will be.

3. Get creative. Sex can mean a lot of different things. Take your time, and realize that not every time needs to end in penetration. There can still be a lot of touching, a lot of words, and a lot of fun.

4. Talk—a lot. Ask each other what is working, what would be best for you to do, what would be best for him to do, etc.

5. Schedule sex. When you are having a date night, plan ahead and make sure that along with the appetizer, your husband can take his medication, so that by the time you get home, sex is the first thing on the agenda.

6. Remind him (often) that he is more than enough man for you.

—Kathi Lipp

More Tips from
Real Hot Mamas

We refuse to get our sex tips from people who don't know about sex.

That's why we won't read the sex tips in most women's magazines or on the internet. (Except, of course, Christian sex websites like those run by our experts.) We're not being judge-y, but when a twenty-year-old single girl is giving us tips on how to connect with our husbands in a meaningful way, we just can't trust what she has to say.

Our hot mama friends, on the other hand, we trust completely.

These women know what God desires for our sex lives. And they are willing to stand in the gap with us and fight for strong marriages. Plus, our hot mama friends are among the hippest, coolest, and most fun girls we know, so we can't help but want to glean all sorts of good advice from them.

With all this in mind, we thought we would finish this book on a high note—so we asked our brave hot mama friends to share their hottest and flirtiest sex tips with us. And we're sharing them with you. So, without further ado, here is the ultimate, most comprehensive list of sex tips from our trusted hot mama friends.

REAL *Hot Mama* IDEAS

"I dedicate an hour one morning every week to my husband (this may have to occur very early, but he doesn't mind). I give him a foot massage, make him breakfast, and wake him up early with sex. He never minds getting up before the alarm clock."—M

"An older missionary friend once told me that nudity is a wife's best friend. She told me that anytime I feel disconnected from my husband, my first step should be to strip down."—C

"We have a music system in our house, so before sex, I always remember to turn it on. Nothing like soft romantic music piped into your bedroom to 'do the trick.' I always say dancing and music are as important as foreplay to us!"—T

"I had my husband do a sexy photo shoot of me modeling all of my lingerie."—N

"Fight naked. It's pretty hard to stay angry when you're not wearing any clothes."—C

"One night after a great date night, my husband and I laid down the seats in the back of our minivan and had sex in the driveway. We hardly could pay the babysitter before we were kissing again."—T

"On those days when I'm feeling totally exhausted and totally unsexy, I put on a sexy bra and panties under my clothes. It's just enough to remind me that I am a hot mama . . . and by the end of the day, I almost always want to have sex."—I

"Have make-up sex. I used to not get it. I used to think that I couldn't possibly be sexual with him so close to being angry. Now I know better."—D

"Agree to just a back rub. If you still don't want to have sex at the end, that's fine. You'll go to sleep having enjoyed a nice back rub. But, more times than not, a back rub is just enough to help me relax and get into the mood."—I

"Coconut oil. I slather it everywhere before sex—on my arms, on my back, on my lips, on my . . . well, you get the picture. It smells great and it makes everything work smoothly."—C

"We used to have all these secret code words and gestures that meant sex. But in the last few months, I've been just coming right out and saying it. 'Hey, let's have sex' is so much simpler and in its own way, sexier."—I

"Focus, focus, focus. I close my eyes when we're having sex and focus on the sensations I'm feeling. I know it sounds carnal, but oh how good it feels."—Q

Continuing Your Hot Mama Journey

We believe that your marriage can be everything that God intended it to be—romantic, fun, intimate, and hot. And we pray that between the covers of this book you found the inspiration you need to pursue your husband wholeheartedly and the how-tos to get you there in hot mama style. But a happy, healthy, and God-honoring marriage is something you should be working on every minute of every day, so we'd like to invite you to join Team Hot Mama and continue to build a sizzling-hot marriage. Here are a few things you can do:

Head to our Facebook page (www.facebook.com/hotmama guides) and join up with other hot mamas to get the latest on sex, fashion, marriage, and more.

If you haven't already done so, check out our three Hot Mama Challenge ebooks. (Get click-through links at www.hotmamabook.com.) These short ebooks each include ten fun hot mama challenges that will get your sex life sizzling in no time.

If you'd like to study *Hot Mama* or take any of our Hot Mama challenges with your MOPS or small group, head to www.hotmamabook.com to download a free discussion guide. (Because friends don't let friends have a stagnant, boring marriage.)

Join us every week at www.youvegotthispodcast.com as we talk about life, love, marriage, kids, and more on our podcast.

Email us and tell us what you're thinking. Erin can be reached at erin@christianmamasguide.com, and Kathi can be reached at kathi@kathilipp.com.

Wishing you a Hot Mama day!

Notes

Chapter 3 Confidence Is Key

1. Jay Dee, "Is My Spouse Attracted to Me?" Sex Within Marriage, September 21, 2013, http://sexwithinmarriage.com/2013/09/spouse-attracted/. Used with permission by owner and author Jay Dee.

Chapter 11 Heat Things Up

1. Kathi Lipp, *Happy Habits for Every Couple* (Eugene, OR: Harvest House, 2015), 151.

Kathi Lipp is the author of *Praying God's Word for Your Husband, Praying God's Word for Your Life, I Need Some Help Here!, The Husband Project, The Me Project, The Get Yourself Organized Project*, and several other books. Kathi's articles have appeared in dozens of magazines, and she is a frequent guest on *Focus on the Family* radio and TV. She and her husband, Roger, are the parents of four young adults in San Jose, California. Kathi shares her story at retreats, conferences, and women's events across the United States. Connect with her at www.KathiLipp.com, on Facebook at www.facebook.com/AuthorKathiLipp, or on Twitter @KathiLipp.

Erin MacPherson is the author of *Free to Parent, The Christian Mama's Guide to Having a Baby, The Christian Mama's Guide to Baby's First Year, The Christian Mama's Guide to Parenting a Toddler*, and *The Christian Mama's Guide to the Grade School Years*. In addition to writing books, Erin cohosts the *So Here's the Thing* podcast with Kathi Lipp and stays busy speaking on the MOPS circuit, appearing on various radio shows and podcasts, and writing for magazines like *Thriving Family* and *MomSense*. She is the mom to three young kids—Joey (age 9), Kate (age 7), and Will (age 3)—and is married to Cameron, who is an assistant principal at a big public Texas high school. Connect with Erin at www.christian mamasguide.com, on Facebook at www.facebook.com/christ ianmamasguide, or on Twitter @emacphe.

Connect with
Kathi & Erin

KathiLipp.com   ChristianMamasGuide.com

kathi   erin

For every overwhelmed mom—
there is **HELP** and **HOPE**.

Tools to Pray for Your Husband and Yourself
with **PURPOSE** and **POWER**

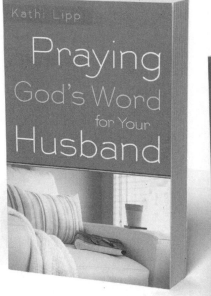

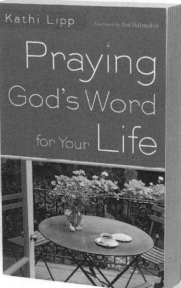